I0140550

Abstracts of the

Orphans Court Proceedings

of

HARFORD COUNTY
MARYLAND

1778-1800

Henry C. Peden, Jr., M.A.

HERITAGE BOOKS
2008

HERITAGE BOOKS
AN IMPRINT OF HERITAGE BOOKS, INC.

Books, CDs, and more—Worldwide

For our listing of thousands of titles see our website
at
www.HeritageBooks.com

Published 2008 by
HERITAGE BOOKS, INC.
Publishing Division
100 Railroad Ave. #104
Westminster, Maryland 21157

Originally published 1990

All rights reserved. No part of this book may be reproduced or
transmitted in any form or by any means, electronic or mechanical,
including photocopying, recording or by any information storage
and retrieval system without written permission from the author,
except for the inclusion of brief quotations in a review.

International Standard Book Numbers
Paperbound: 978-1-58549-175-9
Clothbound: 978-0-7884-7730-0

INTRODUCTION

The information contained in this book was abstracted from the original book found in the Register of Wills Office in Bel Air, Harford County, Maryland, entitled "Orphans Court Docket, 1778-1797." The title is a bit misleading as it contains the actual records of the court proceedings from February, 1778 to January, 1800.

These old dockets and proceedings of the Orphans Court contain genealogical information that may not be found anywhere else in the courthouse. Many entries pertain to the apprenticeship of children (referred to as orphans even though one of their parents may be still alive) who were "bound out" to someone to learn a trade or craft for a designated period of time, or until reaching a certain age (21 for boys and 16 for girls). Oftimes, both their age and birth date are given, as well as a parent's name. Many are listed in the settling of the estate, oftimes naming their parents, siblings, and other relatives. In some cases respectable citizens were appointed by the court to act in settling matters in dispute, and in many instances the real property of the deceased (land, houses, improvements) is fully described in the record. Most disputes pertain to the complaints filed against family members and interested parties for not settling and distributing the estate in a timely manner.

Comparable information for the period prior to 1777 can be found records of the Prerogative Court of Maryland found at the Maryland State Archives in Annapolis. Following the Orphans Court Docket Book which ends circa 1800, are the General Entries Books held by the Register of Wills Office in Bel Air which contain similar information beginning in 1800.

Henry C. Peden, Jr.

ABSTRACTS OF THE ORPHANS COURT PROCEEDINGS
HARFORD COUNTY, MARYLAND, 1778-1800

FEBRUARY COURT, 1778
Court Justices: AQUILA HALL, AQUILA PACA and JOHN LOVE.
LUKE GRIFFITH, administrator of MARY GRIFFITH, agst. EDWARD WARD
    and wife.
HENRY VANSICKLE, administrator of GARRETT GARRETSON, agst.
    RICHARD GARRETSON.
Application of JOHN PATTERSON for subpoena to be issued for
    JOHN LEE WEBSTER regarding the estate of JOSEPH BUTLER.
MARTHA PRESBURY, admx. of WILLIAM ROBINSON PRESBURY.

APRIL COURT, 1778
HUGH BAY agst. JAMES HOLMES, regarding JOHN BAY's estate.
JAMES KENNEDY, adm. of JOHN MONTGOMERY agst. MATTHEW
    McCLINTICK, and another case agst. JOHN TOWNSLEY.
Court Justices: AQUILA HALL, AQUILA PACA, JOHN LOVE.
HUGH BAY agst. THOMAS KENNEDY regarding JOHN BAY's estate.

JUNE COURT, 1778
WILLIAM GRAFTON appointed guardian to RACHEL JEWEL, orphan of
    ROBERT JEWEL, deceased.
JOHN ROBERTSON appointed guardian to MARGARET JEWEL, orphan of
    ROBERT JEWEL, deceased.
WILLIAM MORRIS, orphan of JOHN MORRIS, aged 17 years on the
    fourth day of January, 1778, bound as apprentice to JONATHAN
    WOOLAND to learn the trade of weaver and to read, write and
    cipher as far as the rule of three.
SAMUEL GRIFFITH requested an estimate of the value of the real
    estate of GEORGE GARRETSON, deceased. The Court appointed
    WILLIAM SMITH (Bayside) & GREENBERRY DORSEY.
EDWARD WARD, JR. agst. LUKE GRIFFITH. Case was dismissed.
MICAJAH DEAVER, adm. of SUSANNA KIMBLE, deceased, agst. JOHN
    KIMBLE, regarding the goods & chattels of the deceased.

AUGUST COURT, 1778
JOHN CROW, being 13 years of age the 27th of March, 1778, by his
    own consent, bound to JAMES DANIEL to learn to be a farmhand
    & to read, write & cipher as far as rule of 3.
RACHEL JOHNSON, administratrix of WILLIAM JOHNSON, summoned
    regarding the estate balance. (Case also mentions JACOB BULL
    and BENJAMIN AMOS, of James).
WILLIAM GRAFTON agst. SARAH GRAFTON in a case regarding the
    administration of the estate of WILLIAM GRAFTON, her late
    husband.

SEPTEMBER COURT, 1778
JOHN ALLRIGHT, being 5 years of age the 11th of March, 1778,
    bound to WILLIAM GIBSON to learn to be a farmer, and to
    learn to read, write & cipher as far as the rule of 3.
MARGARET YOUNG, orphan of ROBERT YOUNG, bound to JOSEPH ROSE
    (ROASE) until age 16, which will be on August 7, 1786, to
    learn to read (with the usual freedoms at age 16).
ROBERT JONES, age 17 on February 27, 1779, bound to WILLIAM WOOD
    to learn to be a weaver and to read, write and cipher as far
    as the rule of three.

1

MARY McGENNES, age 4 on July 10, 1778, bound to ROBERT HUNT until
    she is 16, and to be taught to read distinct.
EDWARD CANTWELL COLLINS, age 10 on December 16, 1778, bound to
    THOMAS AYRES until age 21, and is to be taught to read,
    write and cipher as far as the rule of three.
GARRETT GARETSON agst. ELIJAH BLACKSTON, regarding the orphans of
    EDWARD GARRETSON, deceased.

NOVEMBER COURT, 1778
Justices: AQUILA HALL, AQUILA PACA, JOHN LOVE, JOHN RUMSEY.
WILLIAM WILSON appointed to appraise negroes belonging to
    the estate of NATHANIEL GILES.
JACOB GILES, JR. appointed guardian to HANNAH GILES, SARAH
    GILES, ELIZABETH GILES, and CAROLINE GILES, orphans of
    the estate of NATHANIEL GILES, deceased.
THOMAS LAMDEN was discharged from his former master STEPHEN
    NORTON and bound to JOHN BESHONG to be a shoemaker and to
    read, write and cipher as far as the rule of three.
SARAH SMITHSON, widow of THOMAS SMITHSON, appointed guardian
    to her infant son THOMAS SMITHSON, with the securities
    being MARTIN PRESTON and DANIEL THOMPSON.
WILLIAM SMITH (Bayside) and THOMAS GILES approved securities
    for the estate of NATHANIEL GILES, deceased.
LUKE GRIFFITH, adm. of MARY GRIFFITH, agst. EDWARD WARD, JR.
    (Court ordered witnesses examined by interrogatories.)
SARAH GRAFTON still in contempt over not administering the
    estate of her late husband, WILLIAM GRAFTON.

DECEMBER COURT, 1778
BENJAMIN GARRETSON and JAMES GARRETSON, orphans of EDWARD
    GARRETSON, chose their brother GARRETT GARRETSON as
    their guardian. Court approved HENRY VANSICKLE and JOHN
    RUFF as securities. (Bond entered January 20, 1779.)
Court ordered Letters of Administration to SAMUEL GRAFTON to
    administer his father's estate (WILLIAM GRAFTON).

FEBRUARY COURT, 1779
Justices: AQUILA PACA, JOHN RUMSEY, JOHN LOVE, THOS. JOHNSON
JOHN BOWDEY, aged 15 in July, 1778, bound himself to ROBERT
    COOK until age 21 to learn the trade of a weaver.
GEORGE RYLIE, aged 14 on Aril 5, 1779, bound by Court to
    JOHN FORWOOD until age 21 to learn the art of millary
    and the business of farming, and to read, write and
    cipher as far as the rule of three.
BENJAMIN RYLIE, age 12 on May 1, 1779, bound by Court until
    age 21, to JOHN FORWOOD to learn the art of millary and
    farming, and read, write, cipher to the rule of three.
CYRUS BILLINGSLEY and THOMAS HOPE appointed securities for
    the performance of ELIZABETH WATKINS, admx. of JOHN
    WATKINS, as Trustee for the children's estate.
Court appointed JOSHUA DURHAM and HESY GREEN to estimate the
    value of the real estate of JOHN JOHNSON, deceased.

JUNE COURT, 1779
DANIEL REARDON, aged 6 on May 15, 1779, bound until age 21
    to JAMES CALASPY to learn the farming business and to
    read, write and cipher as far as the rule of three.
JOHN ROASE, aged 19 on May 15, 1779, bound himself until age

21 to JOHN JACKSON to learn the trade of a weaver.
By order of the Court, SAMUEL GRIFFITH and GEORGE PATTERSON
    entered on the lands of GARRETT GARRETSON of New Park, late
    of Harford County, on May 23, 1778, and found the plantation
    in this state: a log dwelling house 16 feet square with
    shingle roof and brick chimney, plank floor above and below;
    an old kitchen 20 feet long, in very bad repair; a log
    quarter 16 feet long, in bad repair and log barn thirty-six
    feet long by eighteen feet wide in bad repair; log corn
    house fifteen feet long by ten feet wide in bad repair; an
    old log house sixteen feet square in very bad repair; 95
    apple trees, peach trees, 4 cherry trees, 1 walnut tree,
    fence rails, and 5 acres of meadow; estimated yearly value
    of 20 pounds.
JOHN ARCHER appeared and qualified as Orphans Court Justice.
CHARLES HANBY, aged 10 on January 1, 1779, bound to JACOB
    FORWOOD, until age 21, to learn the farming business.
MARTHA AMOSS, orphan of JOSHUA AMOSS, chose GEORGE VOGAN as
    her guardian (age not given).
Court appointed JOHN LOVE and WILLIAM BULL as Trustees to
    pay off the estate of EDMUND BULL in accordance with
    the terms of his wife SUSANNA BULL, his executrix.

AUGUST COURT, 1779
Court Justices: AQUILA PACA, JOHN LOVE, JOHN RUMSEY, THOMAS
    JOHNSON and JOHN ARCHER.
JOHN COOK, age 16 on May 1, 1778, bound to GILBERT JONES,
    until age 21, to learn to be a cabinet joyner and to
    read, write and cipher as far as the rule of three.
Court appointed MATTHEW TALBOTT and THOMAS ENSOR securities
    for JAMES TALBOTT, duly making up with and settling the
    estate of JOHN CLAYTON, deceased, which estate had been
    administered on by the widow of said Clayton, who had
    entered into a bond with DAVID LEE and ISAIAH LINTON to
    THOMAS JONES, then Deputy Commissery, for duly admin.
JOSEPH ROBINSON, aged 7 on March 9, 1780, bound until age 21
    to JOHN HANNAH to learn the weaving trade.
JOSHUA BENNETT, aged 8 on April 5, 1780, bound to JAMES DREW
    to learn the farming business.
ANN GRIFFITH, aged......on June 10, 1779, bound to MARGARET
    AKINS until age 16, and to learn to read and write.
MORDECAI GRIFFITH, aged 5 years on December 25, 1779, bound
    to JAMES NORRIS until age 21, and to learn the sadlers
    trade, and to read, write and cipher to the rule of 3.
JOHN GRIFFITH, aged 3 on November 25, 1779, bound to THOMAS
    TURNER until age 21 to learn the weavers trade and to
    read, write and cipher as far as the rule of three.
MARY SHORT, age 4 on September 14, 1779, bound to SAMUEL
    BEARD until age 16, and to learn to read and write.
JESSE TAYLOR, age 15 on March 20, 1780, by his own consent, bound
    to ABRAHAM TAYLOR until age 21 to learn the trade of
    shoemaker, and to read, write and cipher as far as the rule
    of three.
JOHN McMULLON, aged.....on May 27, 1780, bound to (name not
    stated) until 21, and to learn the trade of blacksmith.
ANN JOHNSON, widow of JOHN JOHNSON, appointed guardian to
    her son JAMES JOHNSON.
AQUILA MASSEY chose JONATHAN WOODLAND as his guardian, with
    SAMUEL GROOM OSBORN and JOHN HAMMOND DORSEY securities.
AMOSS JAMES and WILLIAM JAMES chose MAULDEN AMOSS as their

guardian, with JOHN TAYLOR, Esq. and SAMUEL CALDWELL as
securities approved by the Court.
SARAH YOUNG, aged......bound until age 16 to WILLIAM GAIL to
learn to read and write.
MARY JONES, daughter of JAMES JONES, aged 8 on May 14, 1780,
bound to MARY JONES, daughter of JOHN JONES, and to learn to
read and write.
JACOB WHEELER appointed guardian to SUSANNA LUSBY & CLEMENCY
HUGHES LUSBY, with THOMAS WHEELER and THOMAS BLANEY as
securities approved by the Court.
JOHN THOMAS, aged 14 in November, 1779, bound to JOHN BULL,
with the consent of his father, until 21, to learn the
trade of blacksmith, and to learn to read and write so
as to do his own business.
MARK McGOVERON chose ABRAHAM WHITEACRE as his guardian, with
MORDECAI AMOS SR. and WILLIAM AMOS (of Joshua) approved
as securities by the Court.
EDWARD DAY (OF EDWARD) and LAMBERT WILMORE appointed by the
Court to estimate the yearly value of the real estate
of AQUILA MASSEY, orphan of JONATHAN MASSEY, deceased.
Court appointed GREENBERRY DORSEY and GEORGE PATTERSON to
divide the estate of BENJAMIN GARRETSON, orphan of
EDWARD GARRETSON, amongst his representatives.
WILLIAM McCARTY, aged 13 on September 5, 1779, bound until
21 to DANIEL DONOVAN to learn the trade of shoemaker.

FEBRUARY COURT, 1780
WILLIAM ROBINSON, aged 14 on August 30, 1779, was bound to
21 to PETER CARROLL to learn the shoemaking trade, and
to read, write and cipher as far as the rule of three.
CHARLES ROBINSON, aged 12 on August 30, 1779, bound until
age 21 to JOSIAS HITCHCOCK to learn the blacksmith's
trade and to read, write and cipher to the rule of 3.
WILLIAM CAMBPELL, aged 12 on October 1, 1779, bound until
age 21 to JAMES GILES to learn the farming business and
to read, write and cipher as far as the rule of three.
WILLIAM SCOTT, aged 12 in May, 1780, bound until age 21 to
FREDERICK FRAILEY to learn the blacksmith's trade and
to read, write and cipher as far as the rule of three.
SAMUEL McCARTY, aged 16 on December 22, 1780, bound with the
consent of his mother to JOHN ANTILL to learn the trade
of weaving and to read, write, cipher to the rule of 3.
JACOB DEBRULAR, aged 10 on March 29, 1780, bound with the
consent of his mother to BENJAMIN HARBERT to learn the
trade of weaving, and to learn to read, write, and
cipher as far as the rule of three.
LEVY SPRINGER McCARTY, aged 8 on October 5, 1780, bound with
the consent of his mother to JACOB DONNOVAN until age
21 to learn the trade of shoemaker, and to learn to
read, write and cipher as far as the rule of three.
THOMAS BROOKS, aged 7 on January 8, 1780, bound with the
consent of his mother to HENRY THOMAS until age 21 to
learn the trade of farming plough making business, and
to read, write and cipher as far as the rule of three.
RICHARD COOP, aged 16 on April 23, 1780, bound with the
consent of his father to MATTHEW McKLEHANEY until age
21 to learn to be a taylor, and nine month's schooling.

MARY SHORT, aged 6 on May 1, 1780, bound with the consent of her father to ROBERT CRISWELL until age 16 and to learn to read distinct.

MICHAEL FORD, aged 6 in September, 1780, bound until age 21 to ROBERT CRISWELL to learn the farming business, and to read, write and cipher as far as the rule of three.

JAMES LONEY, aged 3 on June 15, 1780, bound until age 21 to JOHN RUCKMAN according to the prayer of his (Loney's) mother to learn the trade of house carpenter and joiner and to read, write and cipher as far as rule of three.

JOHN PRITCHET, aged 16 on October 8, 1779, bound at his own request to WILLIAM LUCKEY to learn the trade of linnen wheel making, and four month's schooling, and at the end of four years Pritchet will receive a new suit of apparel and a set of turning tools fit for linnen wheel making, and said Pritchet is obliged to work only three month's each year in the plantation business.

Court appointed WILLIAM SMITH and GREENBERRY DORSEY to enter the lands and plantation of MR. GEORGE GARRETSON, late of Harford County, to make a just estimate of an annual value on April 6, 1779; duly qualified before MR. JAMES GILES. Tract known as "Oakington" contained 300 acres with improvements: brick dwelling house in bad repair; brick kitchen in bad repair; one log quarter without a chimney; one good log barn with sheds; one log house; one good log still (stilt?) house; one good garden and vineyard in pretty good repair; 300 rails; 100 apple trees, many of them now decaying; 30 old peach trees and pear trees; one English walnut tree; the above with improvements is estimated to have a 50 lb. yearly rent. Another tract called "The Grove" contained 250 acres on which is a small dwelling, framed, a log kitchen, one log barn with sheds, one log quarter, a log meat house, many thousands of fence rails, 95 apple trees and 30 peach trees; estimated yearly rent of 12 lbs. 10 sh.

MARY BUSSEY, wife of EDWARD BUSSEY, made oath to the Court that negroes Daft, Fanney, Ruth, Mark and Bobb, all the property of THOMAS BUSSEY deceased, have all died since their master. JOHN OFIELD stated he was living with SUSANNA BUSSEY, widow of THOMAS BUSSEY, and saw these negroes in their sickness & after they died he assisted in burial. Sworn before ROBERT AMOSS, March 27, 1780.

JOHN FISHER, aged 16 on December 2, 1780, bound until age 21 to JAMES WALKER to learn the tanner and currier trade.

JUNE COURT, 1780
THOMAS PERRY, aged 6 (no birth date given), bound until age 21 to THOMAS HENLEY to learn to read, write and cipher as far as the rule of three.

JOHN AYRES, aged 11 (no birth date given), bound until age 21 to JOHN NORRIS to learn the trade of shoemaker and to read, write and cipher as far as the rule of three.

AUGUST COURT, 1780
EDWARD BLANEY appointed as guardian of CLEMENCY HUGHS LUSBY, with THOMAS BLANEY and JOSHUA CHALK as securities.

WILLIAM DOOLEY, aged 17 on January 10, 1780, bound until age 21 to JAMES CARROLL, JR. to learn the carpenter's trade and to read, write and cipher as far as rule of three.

THOMAS BUCKINGHAM appointed as guardian of ZACHARIAH AMOSS

and ELIZABETH AMOSS, with BENJAMIN AMOSS and JOHN AMOSS
as securities.
JOHN AMOSS appointed guardian of ELIJAH AMOSS, orphan son of
BENJAMIN AMOSS, with SAMUEL CARLILE and BENJAMIN AMOSS
as securities.
CASIAH DOOZANS "binds her son SOLOMON ARMSTRONG," aged 15 on
September 15, 1780, to MATTHIAS LYNCH until age 21 and
to learn the carpenter and joyner's trade, and to read,
write and cipher as far as the rule of three.
SAMUEL PRITCHETT, aged 17 in September, 1780, bound himself
with the consent of his father, to JOSEPH ROSE to learn
the carpenter and joyner's trade, and to give him three
month's day schooling and three month's night schooling
and to give him wearing apparel upon reaching age 21.
RACHEL DEAVER, aged 12 (no birth date given), bound until 16
to HENRY RUFF (tanner), and to learn to read and write.
JANE CLARK, aged 6 on March 1, 1781, bound to CHARLES BEVARD
until age 16, and to learn to read and write.

OCTOBER COURT, 1780
SUSANNA MORRIS, aged 9 (no birth date given), bound until 16
to BENJAMIN EVERIST, and to learn to read distinct.
EDWARD COLLINS, aged 11 (no birth date given), bound until
age 21 to JOHN COLLINS, and to learn to read, write and
cipher as far as the rule of three.
HANNAH COLLINS, aged 9 (no birth date given), bound until 16
to JOHN COLLINS, and to learn to read distinct.
JOHN HARDEN, aged 9 on February 17, 1781, bound until age 21
to JOHN THOMAS at the request of his mother to learn,
as far as he can, the framing and carpenter's business.
JOSEPH THOMAS, aged 14 in January, 1781, bound until age 21
to HENRY RUFF with the consent of his father, to learn
the tanner and currier's trade, and to read, write and
cipher as far as the rule of three.
SAMUEL McCARTY chose, in court, JOHN ANTIL as his guardian.
Security: WILLIAM HALL (Swan Town) and BENJAMIN EVRIST.
GEORGE BENNETT, aged 5 on May 13, 1781, bound until 21 to
JOHN BULL (blacksmith), and to learn to read, write and
cipher as far as the rule of three.

NOVEMBER COURT, 1780
ABRAHAM DOOZANS, aged 18 on November 3, 1780, bound until 21
to HENRY RUFF to learn the tanner and currier's trade,
as consented to by his (Doozan's) father.
AMOSS GARRETT, aged 16 on July 22, 1780, bound until 21 to
JONATHAN JENKINS to learn the trade of wheat or duck
linen making, linnen wheels, etc., and to learn to read
and write and cipher as far as the rule of three.
JOHN LONG, JR. appointed as guardian of CASSANDRA SCOTT,
orphan of DANIEL SCOTT (of James), with MORDECAI AMOSS
and WILLIAM COAL (COALE) as securities.
RUTH BROWN, said to be aged 8, bound until age 16 to GABRIEL
PETERSON VANHORN to learn to read & write intelligibly.

DECEMBER COURT, 1780
Justices JOHN LOVE, THOS. JOHNSON, JOHN RUMSEY, JOHN ARCHER.
WILLIAM RICHARDSON, BENJAMIN RICHARDSON, SAMUEL RICHARDSON,
JAMES NORRIS (Indian), and ROBERT HAWKINS agst. GEORGE

BRADFORD, Executor of SARAH BOND. Court would not admit
a copy of Sarah Bond's will in the late perorogative
office of this State to be given as evidence. The Jury
found for the plaintiff, GEORGE BRADFORD. Motion to
appeal to the Court of Chancery was granted.
WILLIAM ROBINSON, aged 14 in October, 1780, bound until 21
   to WALTER TAYLOR to learn the weaver trade, and to read
   and write and cipher as far as the rule of three.
RICHARD JAMES, aged 15 on October 1, 1780, bound until 21 to
   SEDGEWICK JAMES to learn the shoemaker trade, and to
   read, write and cipher as far as the rule of three.
STOCKETT JACKSON, aged 10 (no birth date given), bound until
   age 21 to DANIEL RICHARDSON to learn the trade of house
   joiner, and to read, write and cipher to the rule of 3.
AQUILA TAYLOR, aged 18 on August 7, 1780, bound until 21 to
   JOHN MITCHELL to learn the millwright trade.
Court released EDWARD HANSON from his charge of apprentice
   AQUILA PIKE and any further damage he may be charged.
Court appointed THOMAS BOND, JR. and ABRAHAM WHITAKER, Esq.
   to distribute the Estate of BENJAMIN AMOSS, deceased.
Court appointed JAMES MOORE and BENNET MATHEWS to distribute
   the Estate of EDMUND BULL amongst the representatives.

FEBRUARY COURT, 1781
ANN VANSICKLE, aged about 7 years, bound until age 16 to
   DANIEL NORRIS, and to learn to read intelligibly.
THOMAS DEAVER, aged 15 in September, 1780, bound until age
   21 to JOSEPH ROSE (farmer) to learn the carpenter and
   joiner's trade, and to receive six month's schooling.
JAMES HARE, aged 17 on January 2, 1781, bound for 4 years
   to JAMES HANNAH (weaver) to learn his trade and to give
   him ten month's schooling.
WILLIAM PRESBURY, aged 15 on March 7, 1781, bound until 21
   to JOSEPH BILLINGS (silversmith) to learn the trade of
   clock and watchmmaker, and to read, write and cipher as
   far as the rule of three.
JOHN BENNETT, aged about 15, bound until age 21 to NATHAN
   LITTLE to learn the trade of tanner and currier, and to
   read, write and cipher as far as the rule of three.
Court appointed JOHN LOVE and WILLIAM BULL to settle a final
   account of the Estate of EDMUND BULL, deceased.
MARY McNAMARA, aged 5 (no birth date given), bound until 16
   to JOHN GIBSON, and to learn to read distinct.
WILLIAM CAMPBELL, aged 13 (no birth date given), bound until
   age 21 to JAMES MOORE to learn the trade of shoemaker,
   and to read, write and cipher to the rule of three.

APRIL COURT, 1780
JAMES MOOBERRY, aged 11 in February, 1781, bound with the
   consent of his mother, to GEORGE VANDERGRIFT to learn
   the trade of cabinetmaker, and to read, write and cipher as
   far as the rule of three.
Court relieved DANIEL DONNOVAN from any engagement he was
   under to his apprentice WILLIAM McCARTY. Court bound
   WILLIAM McCARTY to AQUILA KEEN on the same terms he
   was bound to DANIEL DONNOVAN to be a blacksmith.
NICHOLAS HORNER, aged 17 on August 15, 1780, bound until 21
   to MATTHIAS LYNCH to learn the trade of carpenter and

joiner, and to receive three month's schooling.

JUNE COURT, 1780
Court ordered the distribution of the Estate of ROBERT LUSBY
now in the hands of the executrix.
EDMUND EDWARDS, aged 16 on February 12, 1781, bound by his
own consent to MOSES DILLION until age 21 to learn the
trade of stone mason, and to read, write and cipher as
far as the rule of three.
MICHAEL LINSEY, aged 11 on March 1, 1781, bound until age 21
to JAMES CREITON to learn the weaving trade and to read
and write and cipher as far as the rule of three.
Court appointed MAJOR SAMUEL SMITH and JAMES WALKER to make
an estimation of the yearly value of the real estate of
JOSEPH FORWOOD, deceased, and return it to the Court.
SOLOMON AGAN chose ABRAHAM REESE for his guardian "to give
five hundred pounds penalty." Securities were JOHN MAHON
and GREGORY BARNS.
Court appointed CHARLES BAKER and WILLIAM DITTO to make an
estimation of the yearly value of the real estate of
SOLOMON AGAN with one of the Justices of the Peace.

SEPTEMBER COURT, 1781
THOMAS DAWSON BANNISTER, aged 12 on August 1, 1781, bound to
CORNELIUS CASHMAN until age 21 to learn the trade of
leather breeches making, and to learn to read, write
and cipher as far as the rule of three.
MARY SHORES, aged 5 on August 3, 1781, bound until age 16 to
JOHN THOMAS, and to read, write, spin, knit and sew.
PARKER HALL, aged 16 in March, 1781, bound until age 21 to
FRANCIS HOLLAND to learn the trade of a carpenter.
REBECCA ELLIOTT, aged 7, bound until age 16 to NICHOLAS POOR
and SARAH POOR, to learn to read intelligibly, and to
learn to spin, knit and do other housewifery business.

JANUARY COURT, 1782
ROBERT AMOSS and CHARLES BAKER certified to the court that they
had divided the lands of SAMSON EAGON, deceased, between
THOMAS JAMES who intermarried with the widow of SAMSON EAGON
and administrator on said estate on the one part and ABRAHAM
REESE, guardian for SOLOMON EAGON, the son and heir of the
said SAMSON EAGON, on the other part, to the satisfaction of
both parties, as follows: The lands lying to the north of
the three lines drawn from the end of 96 perches on the
second line of the land called "Better Luck" and ... until
it intersects the line of land called "Browns Lot." (The
outcome was that the widow got 44 acres & the son 93 acres.)
NATHAN HORNER, aged 13 (no birth date given), bound until 21
to WILLIAM DEBRULAR to learn the farming business, and
to read, write and cipher as far as the rule of three.
ROBERT MOOBERRY, aged 10 on December 26, 1780, bound until
age 21 to KIDD MORALL to learn the joiner's trade, and
to read, write and cipher as far as the rule of three.
Court ordered ROBERT CULVER and BENJAMIN CULVER to appear in
court and return an account of the effects of BENJAMIN
CULVER, deceased, to show why there was no inventory.
RICHARD WHITE agst. BENJAMIN CULVER and ROBERT CULVER.
STATE agst. JAMES FORD: Complaint that Negro Sook was set

free legally before the boy Jacob was born.

STATE agst. JAMES DREW. (nature of case not cited)

JAMES BAKER, STEPHEN ROBERTS, and..........McMASTERS were
    summoned by order of BENJAMIN AMOSS' representatives.

JONAS BAYLIS agst. THOMAS RENSHAW and SAMUEL WEBSTER (of
    Samuel) to show cause as to why the estate of THOMAS
    RENSHAW had not been fully settled.

JACOB FORWOOD's summons was postponed until the next court.

JAMES MOOBERRY, aged 13 on February 26, 1782, bound with the
    consent of his mother to GEORGE VANDEGRIFT until 21 to
    learn the joiner's trade, and to read, write and cipher
    as far as the rule of three.

Court ordered JAMES CLENDENNEN to make sale of all of the
    Estate of JOHN DALE, deceased, with negroes excepted.

Court ordered attachment on WILLIAM AMOSS for contempt.

JOHN WHITAKER agst. JACOB FORWOOD, executor of FRANCES
    GARLAND. (nature of case not cited) For defendant:
    EDWARD HALL, GEORGE LYTLE, HOLLIS HANSON. For the
    plaintiff: WILLIAM CHAUNCEY and WILLIAM LUCKEY.

JAMES DREW to show cause why he misused an orphan boy.

STEPHEN ROBERTS and JOHN ROCKHOLD summoned at the request of
    the executrix of BENJAMIN AMOSS, deceased. Rockhold
    appeared and stated he had no account agst. the estate.

FEBRUARY COURT, 1782

WILLIAM McGOVERON chose WILLIAM HILL as his guardian.

The Representatives of HENRY GARLAND agst. JACOB FORWOOD,
    executor. Summoned for the defendant: EDWARD HALL
    and GEORGE LYTLE. For the plaintiff: JAMES HORNER,
    WILLIAM LUCKEY and HOLLIS HANSON.

The Representatives of BENJAMIN THOMAS agst. ALEX. RIGDON,
    appeared. (nature of case not cited)

MAY COURT, 1782

WILLIAM SMITHSON appeared and qualified as a Court Justice.

JUNE COURT, 1782

Justices: JOHN LOVE, THOMAS JOHNSON, and WILLIAM SMITHSON.

DAVID SHA, aged 16 on March 14, 1782, bound until age 21 to
    JOHN BULL to learn the blacksmith trade, and to receive
    two month's schooling. SHA bound by his own consent.

RALPH YARLEY, aged 13 on June 8, 1782, and NATHANIEL YARLEY,
    aged 11 on July 24, 1782, bound until age 21 with the
    consent of their mother, to WILLIAM EDY to learn the
    cooper's trade, and read, write, cipher to rule of 3.

MOSES MAXWELL and JACOB MAXWELL chose BENJAMIN RUMSEY, Esq.
    as their guardian, and the Court approved him.

SAMUEL BAYLIS, aged 14 on April 13, 1782, chose WILLIAM
    COULTER as his guardian and offered WILLIAM RAMSEY and
    THOMAS BOWLES as his securities. Court approved them.

Court appointed WILLIAM COULTER as guardian of BENJAMIN
    BAYLIS, orphan of NATHANIEL BAYLIS, and offered WILLIAM
    RAMSEY and THOMAS BOWLES as securities. Court approved.

JOHN ROGERS, aged 14 on March 4, 1782, bound until age 21 to
    JOSEPH DAVIS to learn the blacksmith trade and to read,
    write and cipher as far as the rule of three.

JOHN JENKINS chose JOHN PEACOCK as his guardian.

Court appointed JAMES HANNAH as guardian to SCOTT BAYLIS,

orphan of BENJAMIN BAYLIS. Securities were JAMES WALKER and JAMES HORNER.
Court ordered the estates of MOSES MAXWELL and JACOB MAXWELL to be delivered by J. BEALE HOWARD, executor of JAMES MAXWELL, father of the said MOSES and JACOB MAXWELL, into the hands of BENJAMIN RUMSEY, their guardian. The Court appointed JOHN DAY (son of Edward) and ALEXANDER COWAN to appraise the estates of said MOSES and JACOB.

AUGUST COURT, 1782
The Administrator De Bonis Non of THOMAS RENSHAW, deceased, agst. THOMAS RENSHAW (of Thomas). (Reason not cited.)
JANE McGAUGH agst. JOHN PERRYMAN, NICHOLAS ALLENDER, and ISAAC HILTON. (Nature of case not cited)
JOHN DURHAM and MARY BAKER agst. AVARILLA SMITH, executrix of SAMUEL SMITH, deceased. Court ordered Avarilla to pay off her own children, and the Court would appoint a guardian for her grandchildren (the children of JOHN WILSON, deceased) for whose estate she is answerable.
Order by the Court for MARTHA McCOMAS and WILLIAM MORGAN, executors of JOSEPH JOHNSON, deceased, to show cause why they have not fully appraised and administered the estate of the deceased. Case discharged by the Court.
JEAN SIMS, aged 13 on November 1, 1781, bound until age 16 to ANDREW HOWLETT to learn to knit, spin and do other housewifery business, and to learn to read distinct.
JAMES MAHON, aged 13 on January 1, 1782, and FRANCIS SIMS, aged 6 on March 25, 1782, both bound until age 21 to GEORGE ANDERSON to learn the weaving trade and to read, write and cipher as far as the rule of three.
AQUILA JOHNSON, aged 9 on March 25, 1782, bound until age 21 to JACOB FORWOOD to learn to read, write and cipher as far as the rule of three (nothing said about a trade).
WILLIAM LAWDER ("his age not known") bound until age 21 to JOHN ADAMS to learn the shoemaker's trade, and to give him six months schooling.
ELIJAH AMOSS chose THOMAS BUCKINGHAM as his guardian and his securities were BENJAMIN AMOSS and JOHN AMOSS.
Court ordered JACOB FORWOOD, executor of FRANCIS GARLAND, to sell a negro boy, who is the property of the deceased, to benefit of the representatives ("for paying costs").
JOHN BEALE HOWARD, executor of CAPT. JAMES MAXWELL, ordered to deliver up the real estate of the said deceased now the property of the orphans MOSES and JACOB MAXWELL, to the guardian BENJAMIN RUMSEY, plus the personal estate.
SARAH HARE, aged 11 on August 15, 1782, bound until age 16 to PAUL CUMMINGS to learn to read distinct and to knit, spin, sew and do other housewifery business.
WILLIAM HILL appointed guardian of JOHN McGOVERON, orphan of WILLIAM McGOVERON. Securities: HUGH BRIERLY and ...
JOSIAS GLOVER, aged 8 on August 31, 1782, bound until age 21 to AQUILA NORRIS to learn the trade of shoemaker and to read, write and cipher as far as the rule of three.
Executrix of BENJAMIN AMOSS agst. Executor of JAMES STEWART (STEWARD). The Court accepted the additional inventory. AQUILA HALL, Esq., council for Stewart's executor, then appealed the case to the General Court.
Court ordered the distribution of the Estate of ROBERT YOUNG

to the legatees as stated in his last will & testament.

SEPTEMBER COURT, 1782
Court gave approval for HENRY THOMAS, administrator of HENRY
    THOMAS, deceased, to sell estate in order to pay debts.
THOMAS HARDEN, aged 5 on October 7, 1782, bound until age 21
    to JOHN SMITH to learn the cooper's trade and to read,
    write and cipher as far as the rule of three.
DANIEL HARE, aged 9 on July 1, 1782, bound until age 21 to
    WILLIAM MARTIN to learn the shoemaker's trade, and to
    read, write and cipher as far as the rule of three.
EDMUND CRADDOCK, aged 17 on September 10, 1782, bound until
    age 21 by his own choice to PATRICK FINNAGAN to learn
    the cooper's trade, to read and write distinct, and to
    receive "a good kitt new coat jackcoat, breeches, and
    two fine shirts, shoes and stockings."
THOMAS SMITH (age not given) formerly bound to THOMAS HENLEY
    and now bound to JAMES BARNETT until age 21 to learn to
    read, write and cipher as far as the rule of three.
Court allowed ELIZABETH AMOSS and WILLIAM AMOSS, admins. of
    JOSHUA AMOSS, to sell part of the estate to pay debts.

DECEMBER COURT, 1782
JANE McGAUGH agst. JOHN PERRYMAN, NICHOLAS ALLENDER, and
    ISAAC HILTON. Court ordered JOHN PERRYMAN and NICHOLAS
    ALLENDER to pay JANE McGAUGH ten pounds for taking and
    detaining ISAAC HILTON, an orphan boy, from her service
    and to pay her five pounds one year from this date, and
    pay her five pounds within one year after that payment.
GEORGE LYTLE and AMOS HOLLIS agst. JAMES OSBORN, Executor of
    WILLIAM OSBORN. Court ordered that JAMES OSBORN, as
    Executor of WILLIAM OSBORN, get two negro children as
    part of the estate of WILLIAM OSBORN in his possession
    by law or otherwise in order for distribution.
THOMAS CUNNINGHAM and Others agst. DANIEL TREDWAY, Executor
    of THOMAS TREDWAY, deceased. Court ordered that DANIEL
    TREDWAY sell the whole estate of the deceased.
STATE agst. JAMES DREW. Summoned JAMES OSBORN. (No return.)

JANUARY COURT, 1783
WILLIAM BOND appeared and qualified as one of the Justices.
ISAAC HILTON, aged 17 (no birth date given), bound until age
    21 to JOHN PERRYMAN to learn the stone mason trade and
    to read, and receive the usual freedoms due at age 21.
THOMAS WALLACE (WILLACE), aged 16 (no birth date), bound to
    JESSE DAWSON until 21 to learn the blacksmith's trade.
RICHARD WHITE agst. BENJAMIN CULVER and ROBERT CULVER. They
    appeared, but "nothing done here."

FEBRUARY COURT, 1783
Justices: JOHN LOVE, THOS. JOHNSON, WM. SMITHSON, WM. BOND.
JOSEPH PRESBURY (of William), aged 15 on May 5, 1783, bound
    until age 21 to JAMES WETHERALL to learn the sadler's
    trade and to receive the usual freedoms due at age 21.
Court appointed BENNETT MATHEWS as guardian of ANN MATHEWS,
    orphan of LEVEN MATHEWS, with JOHN DAY, JR. and JAMES
    MOORE approved as securities.
Court appointed JOHN DAY, JR., as guardian of LEVEN MATHEWS,

orphan of LEVEN MATHEWS, with BENNETT MATHEWS and
LAMBERT WILMORE approved as securities.
Court appointed JOHN DAY, JR., as guardian of ELIZABETH
FILISANE MATHEWS, with LAMBERT WILMORE and BENNETT MATHEWS
approved as securities. (Not stated in the record, but she
was probably an orphan of Leven.)
Court appoints GREENBERRY DORSEY and WILLIAM LONEY to re-
appraise the estate of LEVEN MATHEWS.
Court orders JOHN LOVE, Esq. to appear in court on Feb. 28,
1783 & produce accounts regarding EDMUND BULL's estate.
Court issued citation for MRS. SUSANNA BULL.
Court issued citation for WILLIAM AMOSS to answer complaint
of ELIZABETH AMOSS on settling estate of JOSHUA AMOSS.
Court issued citation for THOMAS RENSHAW.
Court appt. JAMES LITTLE trustee for Estate of LUKE SWIFT.
Court appointed JAMES THOMPSON as guardian for DAVID
McCRACKING and ELIZABETH McCRACKING, with securities
being WILLIAM COULTER and DAVID THOMPSON. Approved.
Court ordered that "the money in MR. ALEX. RIGDON's hand of the
estate of BARNEY CONNOLLY to be settled as in March 1779."
STOCKETT JACKSON, aged 12 on December 12, 1782, bound until
age 21 to MATTHEW DORSEY to learn the taylor's trade
and to read, write and cipher to the rule of three.
JAMES CREIGHTON agst. SUSANNA BULL, Executrix of EDMUND BULL
(nature of case not stated). Account received by court.
ABRAHAM WHITAKER appeared and qualified as a Court Justice.
JOHN MOALTON, aged 17 on February 1, 1783, bound until 21 to
OBEDIAH PRITCHARD to learn the blacksmith's trade and
to receive six month's schooling.
JAMES HAMBY, aged 8 on August 25, 1782* bound until age 21
to WILLIAM EVITT to learn to be a farmer, and to read,
write and cipher as far as the rule of three.
WILLIAM HAMBY, aged 8 on October 25, 1782* bound until 21 to
JONATHAN KNIGHT to learn the farming business, and read
and write and cipher as far as the rule of three.
*Ed. Note: James Hamby and William Hamby were twins. The Court
erred in giving their birth dates as two months apart. They
were born either on August 25th or October 25th, 1782.
(Ref: 1776 Census, Susquehannah Hundred)

MARCH COURT, 1783
Court ordered the Estate of JOSHUA AMOSS be sold so far as
may raise a sum sufficient to pay any debts.
NATHAN GALLION and SAMUEL WEBSTER (of Samuel) agst. THOMAS
RENSHAW (of Thomas). Appeared, but case postponed.
ISAAC WEBSTER to show his account if he has any against the
Estate of PATRICK HENNESEY. Appeared, but nothing done.
JOHN LEE GIBSON to show his account if he has any against
Estate of PATRICK HENNESEY. Appeared, but nothing done.
CORNELIUS CASHMAN agst. SAMUEL LITTON. (Nature not stated)
JOSHUA BENNETT, aged 11 on July 15, 1783, bound until age 21
to WILLIAM BOULSTER to learn the blacksmith's trade and
to read, write and cipher as far as the rule of three.
Court appointed WILLIAM BAKER as guardian of JAMES WILSON,
BENJAMIN WILSON and AVARILLA WILSON, orphans of JAMES
WILSON, with JAMES LEE and WILLIAM WILSON, securities.
Court ordered ISAAC GIBSON and JOHN LEE GIBSON to appear and
show their case against the Estate of PATRICK HENNESEY.

12

Court appointed HOLLIS HANSON as trustee of the Estate of
    JAMES GALLION, deceased, "for the use of the orphans."
Court ordered JAMES CLENDENNEN to render to MARY DALE, widow
    of JOHN DALE, the use of two negro women yearly as long
    as they all shall live, and for JAMES CLENDENNEN to pay
    MARY DALE "five pounds yearly as good as money was at
    the time of JOHN DALE's will was made."

MAY COURT, 1783
Justices: THOMAS JOHNSON, WILLIAM BOND, ABRAHAM WHITAKER and
    WILLIAM SMITHSON.
Court bound BENSHAW, a negro boy aged 8, to SARAH GRAFTON,
    until 21, and to give him the usual freedoms when 21.

JUNE COURT, 1783
WILLIAM McGOVEREN, ward of WILLIAM HILL chose SAMUEL GRAFTON
    guardian. HUGH BRIERLY and WILLIAM GRAFTON, securities.
JAMES WOOD (son of JAMES WOOD, deceased), aged 15, bound to
    JOHN COOLEY until age 21 to learn the house joiner and
    carpenter trade, and read, write & cipher to rule of 3.
ELIZABETH WOOD, aged 11, bound until 16 to WILLIAM RAMSEY to
    learn to read, write, sew, knit, spin and other house-
    wifery business, with the usual freedoms at age 16.
CORNELIUS CASHMAN agst. SAMUEL LITTON. (Did not appear)
STATE agst. JARRETT HOPKINS, JOHN HAWKINS and JAMES FISHER.
    (Nature of case not stated in record; no action taken)
JOHN PAIN, aged 13 on June 1, 1783, bound until age 21 to
    ALEXANDER DUNCAN to learn the shoemaker's trade and to
    read, write and cipher as far as the rule of three.
Court ordered the Estate of EDMUND BULL "be sold in the
    following manner (to wit) the Continental money paid
    away in the course of the administration and the money
    received shall stand one against the other as far as
    paid away and all remaining in the hands of the
    executrix at the real value."

AUGUST COURT, 1783
THOMAS BROWN (BROWNE) chose JOSHUA BROWNE his guardian, with
    SAMUEL GROOM OSBORN and WILLIAM OSBORN as securities.
DAVID SWIFT, aged 12 on January 1, 1783, bound until age 21
    to JAMES LITTLE and to give the boy a year's schooling.
FRANCIS THOMAS, aged 9 on March 8, 1783, bound until age 21
    to BENNET GREEN and to learn to read, write and cipher
    as far as the rule of three.
Court appointed SAMUEL CALDWELL and BENJAMIN B. NORRIS to
    settle a money dispute between the executor of BENJAMIN
    SCOTT, deceased, and CAPT. ROBERT HARRIS.
BENJAMIN HANSON agst. RACHEL GALLION, administratrix of
    JAMES GALLION, deceased. (Did not appear in court)
STATE agst. JARRARD HOPKINS for marrying Ruth (a free woman)
    to a slave. (Did not appear; contempt citation issued)
    JOHN HAWKINS and JAMES FISHER were summoned to testify
    against Hopkins, and they appeared and were examined.

OCTOBER COURT, 1783
Court appointed NATHAN GALLION guardian to JOHN GALLION,
    orphan of JAMES GALLION, with THOMAS JOHNSON and JOHN
    COPELAND approved as securities. Court ordered SAMUEL

GRIFFITH and GREENBERRY DORSEY to appraise said estate
"as shall be the share or dividend of said orphan, the
guardian to sell such part of the said estate as is
perishable (negroes excepted) and the money put to use
for the support of the orphan."
STATE agst. JARRARD HOPKINS. "Contempt, or will show cause
why he married Ruth, a free woman, to a negro slave."
HOLLIS HANSON, administrator of BENJAMIN HANSON agst. RACHEL
GALLION, administratrix of JAMES GALLION. To show why
she did not fully settle and make up Gallion's estate.
JOHN BUCKLEY and wife, against THOMAS GILBERT. Said Gilbert to
answer a certain complaint to be made known in Court
respecting an apprenticed lad's learning.
Citation issued for SEDGEWICK JAMES to answer the complaint
of WILLIAM CANNON. (No return.)

NOVEMBER COURT, 1783
JOHN MASSEY chose ISAAC MASSEY as his guardian, with ISAAC
WEBSTER and JOHN L. WEBSTER approved as securities.
ELIZABETH AMOSS, administratrix of JOSHUA AMOSS, requested
the Court to allow DANIEL TREDWAY as an assistant in
selling the estate of JOSHUA AMOSS, deceased. Court
allowed him and ROBERT HARRIS to act as assistants.
Representatives of RICHARD JAMES against SEDGEWICK JAMES.
CHARLES BAKER and wife, administrators of MAURICE BAKER, to show
cause why they had not fully settled said estate.
Securities: THOMAS SAUNDERS and JOSEPH SAUNDERS. Real
estate yearly value to be estimated by JAMES McCONNOLL
and WILLIAM BOND.

DECEMBER COURT, 1783
HOLLIS HANSON complains the Estate of JAMES GALLION, JR. was
not settled and prayed for a trustee to be appointed;
one was (no name). JOHN RUFF and GEORGE PATTERSON were
appraisers. "Perishable articles of estate to be sold."
Court ordered DANIEL TREDWAY and CAPT. ROBERT HARRIS to sell
such parts of the estate of JOSHUA AMOSS, deceased, as
necessary to pay the debts due by the said deceased.
JOHN TREMAIN, aged 16 on March 15, 1784, bound until age 21
to WILLIAM PRIGG to learn to read, write and cipher as
far as the rule of three.
JAMES SHIELDS, son of JOHN SHIELDS, aged 4 on Oct. 1, 1783,
bound until age 21 to RALPH PILES, JR. to learn to read
and write and cipher as far as the rule of three.
JOHN SHIELDS, son of JOHN SHIELDS, aged 2 in November, 1783,
now a charge to the county, bound to MARY RHODES until
age 21, and to be taught to read and write.
SAMUEL WILSON requested the Court that he be "appointed the
guardian of his infant son, WILLIAM WILSON, to superintend any matter that may be in dispute in respect to
certain land devised to him the said WILLIAM WILSON by
the last will and testament of AQUILA PACA, JR., dec."
CORBIN LEE chose his father JAMES LEE as his guardian "to
superintend his business respecting the land devised
to him by AQUILA PACA, JR.'s last will and testament."

14

FEBRUARY COURT, 1784
THOMAS JEFFERY against HUGH JEFFERY. To show cause why he had
    not administered the Estate of MARTHA JEFFERY.
Citation issued to HUGH KIRKPATRICK to show cause why he had
    not administered the Estate of THOMAS NESBIT (NEASBIT).
HUGH JEFFERY agst. ELIZABETH JEFFERY. (Nature not stated)
Court bound a negro boy named BENNETT, aged 11 on Sept. 15,
    1783, to JOHN FORWOOD until age 21 to learn to read and
    do plantation business, with usual freedoms at age 21.
JOSEPH PRESBURY, orphan of WILLIAM, chose JAMES WETHERALL,
    sadler, as his guardian, with JAMES McCOMAS and JOSEPH
    PRESBURY, of JOSEPH, as securities. Court ordered the
    estate of the said JOSEPH PRESBURY (of William), now in
    the hands of SAMUEL GRIFFITH, Acting Administrator, to
    be delivered and paid to JAMES WETHERALL the guardian.
CORBIN LEE chose JACOB FORWOOD as his guardian, with GABRIEL
    CHRISTIE and JOHN PATTERSON approved as securities.
Court ordered JAMES McCOMAS and JOHN DURHAM to appraise the
    goods and household furniture of JOSHUA BROWNE for his
    brother JOHN THOMAS BROWNE according to father's will.
WILLIAM STANDIFORD, aged 12 on December 10, 1783, bound to
    LANCELOT CARLILE until age 21 to learn the carpenter's
    trade and read, write and cipher to the rule of three.

MARCH COURT, 1784
Justices: JOHN LOVE, THOMAS JOHNSON, WILLIAM SMITHSON,
    WILLIAM BOND and ABRAHAM WHITAKER.
THOMAS JAMES and wife offered CAPT. CHARLES BAKER and ASEL
    HITCHCOCK as securities for the Estate of SAMSON AGAN.
Citation issued against EDWARD PARKER at request of BENNETT
    BUSSEY. (No return.)
Citation issued against THOMAS JAMES at the request of JAMES
    BARTON to give security. Gave security, and discharged.
Citation issued agst. GABRIEL CHRISTIE to show cause why he
    claimed sold property in a vessel which was in part the
    property of AQUILA PACA, deceased. Also summoned were
    GEORGE PATTERSON, EDWARD CARVIL TOLLEY and JOSIAS HALL
    to testify for the plaintiff. Christie did not appear
    and there was no return on those summoned in this case.
LUKE HANSON, aged 16, bound until age 21 to JAMES WALKER to
    learn the tanner and currier's trade.
SAMSON AGAN chose WILLIAM HITCHCOCK as his guardian, with
    ASEL HITCHCOCK and CAPT. CHARLES BAKER as securities.
Court appointed WILLIAM HITCHCOCK as guardian to MARY AGAN,
    CLEMENTINE AGAN, and SARAH AGAN, with ASEL HITCHCOCK
    and CAPT. CHARLES BAKER approved as securities.
Court appointed WILLIAM BRADFORD and RICHARD RUFF to
    appraise the estate remaining for distribution to the
    children of JONATHAN MASSEY, deceased, now in the hands
    of JONATHAN WOODLAND.

APRIL COURT, 1784
Citation issued to SEDGWICK JAMES, executor of RICHARD JAMES
    deceased, to show cause why he had not administered the
    estate fully. (James was given more time to comply.)
Citation issued to JOSEPH JACOB WALLACE and THOMAS WALLACE,
    executors of GRACE WALLACE, to show why the estate of
    the deceased had not been fully settled.

15

State of Maryland empowered BENEDICT EDWARD HALL, JOHN LOVE,
    THOMAS BOND (of THOMAS), JOHN ARCHER and SAMUEL HUGHES,
    or any three of them, to hold court as Justices of the
    Orphan Court of Harford County until duly discharged.
    Signed by WILLIAM PACA. Wit: JOHN ROGERS, Chancellor.

APRIL COURT, 1784
Petition of DANIEL TREDWAY and ROBERT HARRIS, trustees of the
    estate of JOSHUA AMOS, deceased. Also mentions a child (no
    name given) and "a bond given for specie that was original-
    ly given for a continental debt to WILLIAM SPEERS as set
    forth in the said petition."
JOHN HETHCOT CHAMBERLIN, aged 11 on November 17, 1783, bound
    until 21 to MOSES DILLON to learn the stone mason trade
    and read, write and cipher as far as the rule of three.
ROBERT BOYLE, aged 17 on November 16, 1783, bound to JAMES
    MOORE, tanner, for two years and ten months to learn the
    tanner and currier's trade, and "to find him in working
    cloaths during the aforesaid time."
SAMUEL BAYLIS, aged 16 on April 13, 1784, bound until age 21
    to JAMES MOORE to learn the tanner & shoemaker's trade,
    and "to find him working cloaths during this time."
JAMES LENOM, aged 10 on May 19, 1784, bound to PHILIP ALBERT
    until age 21 to learn the shoemaker's trade, and read,
    write and cipher as far as the rule of three.
Court admitted the settlement of the estate of ROBERT YOUNG
    and ordered the executors to pay DANIEL TREDWAY, JR. in
    the amount of 27 pounds, 14 shillings, and 4 pence.
Court ordered on request of MR. ALEXANDER COWAN a citation
    issued to the widow of DR. JOHN DALE, now MARY BUCHANAN
    living in the State of Delaware, served before witness.
Court adjudged that "a vessel in partnership between AQUILA
    PACA, deceased, and GABRIEL CHRISTIE, be struck out of
    the inventory of AQUILA PACA who is since deceased, and
    (that it) remain the property of GABRIEL CHRISTIE."
DANIEL OF ST. THOMAS JENIFER presented the following list of
    "maimed soldiers that have lately received orders on
    the Treasury for two months half pay due them under the
    Act of October Session, 1778. This list I transmit to
    you that they may not again be paid for those months."

BOTTS, JOSEPH	2	lbs.	10 sh.
BURK, JAMES	2	lbs.	10 sh.
BREWER, JAMES	2	lbs.	10 sh.
BUTCHER, JOHN	2	lbs.	10 sh.
DENT, JOHN Corpl.	5	lbs.	10 sh.
DYRE, JAMES	2	lbs.	10 sh.
DUFFY, MICHAEL	2	lbs.	10 sh.
EVANS, WILLIAM	2	lbs.	10 sh.
FINLAYSON, GEORGE	2	lbs.	10 sh.
HAZEL, CALEB	3	lbs.	15 sh.
IRE, FREDERICK	2	lbs.	10 sh.
ISAACS, JAMES	2	lbs.	10 sh.
KEITH, DANIEL	2	lbs.	10 sh.
MACNAMARA,	2	lbs.	10 sh.
MCGEE, THOMAS	2	lbs.	10 sh.
MATHEWS, JOHN Corpl.	5	lbs.	10 sh.
O'HARA, JAMES	2	lbs.	10 sh.
PAPER, JAMES	2	lbs.	10 sh.

16

```
REYNOL, CHRISTOPHER          2 lbs. 10 sh.
SMITH, JAMES                 2 lbs. 10 sh.
ELY, WILLIAM                 2 lbs. 10 sh.
SHAW, JOHN Segt.             3 lbs. 15 sh.
TYNDALL, SAMUEL              2 lbs. 10 sh.
TRITTON, WILLIAM             2 lbs. 10 sh.
WILSON, SAMUEL Segt.         3 lbs. 15 sh.
VANZANT, JOHN                2 lbs. 10 sh.
WILKINSON, RICHARD           2 lbs. 10 sh.
QUINN, JOSEPH                2 lbs. 10 sh.
```

HANNAH CONKLIN, wife of MATTHEW CONKLIN, a guardian to an orphan
    child named MARY FORWOOD, daughter of JOSEPH FORWOOD, late
    of Harford County, requested the Court to have the yearly
    value of the orphan's land estimated so the estate could be
    administered. Court summoned JOHN HAYS and JOHN HANNA "two
    persons of good repute and not being of kin" who had
    entered the 182 acre plantation known as "Widow's Care" on
    August 19, 1782. They swore under oath that they found
    1,012 panels of fence in bad repair composed of about 5,755
    rails; a dwelling house of about 16 feet square; a shop of
    7 feet square in bad repair; a dwelling (new) 15 feet
    square; a spring house 6 feet square; a barn 16 feet wide
    and 20 feet long in midling good repair; and, 13 young
    apple trees. They direct that the guardian put new shingles
    on the roof of the dwelling house, a new clapboard roof on
    the shop and plant 100 apple trees. (Other instructions on
    the care and maintenance of the land were also presented.)
    They determined the yearly rent to be 8 lbs., 15 sh.
Court ordered the executors of ROBERT YOUNG, deceased, to pay
    DANIEL TREDWAY, one of the representatives of the deceased,
    in the amount of 27 lbs., 14 sh., 4 pence.
Attachment of THOMAS WALLIS held over to the next court.
Case of BENNETT BUSSEY against EDWARD PARKER. (No return)
Case of ALEXANDER COWAN agst. MARY BUCHANAN, late MARY DALE,
    executrix of DR. JOHN DALE, dec'd. ("Did Not Appear").
Citation issued to ANN BRYERLY and HENRY BRYERLY, admins. of
    JOHN BRYERLY, deceased, to show cause why they have not
    fully settled his estate ("Longer Time Given").
Citation issued to DANIEL BAYLIS & NATHANIEL BAYLIS, admins.
    of BENJAMIN BAYLIS, deceased, to show cause why they have
    not settled his estate ("Attachment Issued").

JUNE COURT, 1784
ELIZABETH BROADERICK, aged 10 on February 4, 1784, bound to
    age 16 to JAMES MATHERS to be learned to read, and to
    knit, spin, sew and do other housewifery business.
Court stated that an injunction filed by GEORGE BRADFORD in the
    Court of Chancery to stop the proceedings brought by
    WILLIAM RICHARDSON, BENJAMIN RICHARDSON, SAMUEL RICHARDSON,
    JAMES NORRIS and ROBERT HAWKINS, has been dissolved.
    Letters of administration were issued to WILLIAM RICHARDSON
    as one of the nearest of kin to the said SARAH BOND, and
    BENJAMIN B. NORRIS and SEDGWICK JAMES were approved as his
    securities. Court ordered GEORGE BRADFORD to deliver up to
    WILLIAM RICHARDSON all of the effects of SARAH BOND now in
    his possession.
ALEXANDER COWAN appeared and made oath that he showed the
    citation to MARY BUCHANAN, late MARY DALE, and to her
    husband, requesting either of them to appear before the

court to answer his complaint. Neither appeared, so the
court appointed ALEXANDER COWAN trustee of the estate
of DR. JOHN DALE, late of Harford County.
THOMAS BRYERLY, aged 14 and orphan of JOHN BRYERLY, chose
his mother ANN BRYERLY as his guardian. She offered as
security, HENRY BRYERLY and ROBERT BRYERLY (of Thomas).
JESSE WHITLOCK, aged 3 on March 4, 1784, bound until age 21
to JAMES WATSON and to learn to read, write and cipher
as far as the rule of three.
ELIZABETH CRETIN prayed for an order of the Court to make
distribution of the estate of JOHN CRETIN. The Court
appointed IGNATIUS WHEELER & DR. JOHN ARCHER to do so.

AUGUST COURT, 1784
Court Justices: BENEDICT EDWARD HALL, SAMUEL HUGHS, THOMAS
BOND, JOHN LOVE, JOHN ARCHER.
Court ordered GEORGE PRESBURY to give securities for estate
of WILLIAM ROBINSON PRESBURY to the orphans. Appeared,
and JOHN DAY and JOSEPH PRESBURY were approved as such.
Court ordered ANN DURBIN, administratrix of FRANCIS DURBIN,
to answer the complaint of THOMAS DURBIN. She appeared
(and the Court subsequently dismissed the case).
Court ordered HUGH KIRKPATRICK to show cause why he had not
paid the balance of the estate of ROBERT YOUNG to the
"representatives legally claiming."
Court ordered NATHANIEL BAYLIS and DANIEL BAYLIS to answer
the complaint of WILLIAM COULTROUGH to show cause why
they had not settled the estate of BENJAMIN BAYLIS.
Court ordered ROBERT MORGAN to answer the complaint of SARAH
LEWES. Case postponed; "defendant too sick to attend."
Court ordered JAMES SCOTT (of James) to answer the complaint
of ROBERT HARRIS. ("Did not appear; to be renewed.")
Court ordered WILLIAM MORGAN to answer the complaint of
DANIEL McCOMAS & wife. ("To be renewed to next court.")
Court ordered JOHN CAREY to bring JOHN WOOD, orphan of HENRY
WOOD, to court to choose his guardian. ("Appeared, but
nothing done.")
GEORGE BRADFORD prayed for an appeal from the judgment of the
Court. Appeal not granted. Court ordered him to
deliver the effects of SARAH BOND in his possession to
WILLIAM RICHARDSON, administrator of said SARAH BOND.
GEORGE BRADFORD refused. Court ordered an attachment of
GEORGE BRADFORD for contempt and he was committed to
the Sheriff's custody until he complied with the order.
LEONARD WHEELER, orphan of BENJAMIN WHEELER, chose EDWARD
BIVEN as guardian. Security: BENJAMIN & LEONARD GREEN.
Court passed an order to be given on the Treasurer to pay
VALLENTINE SMITH for 11 pounds and 5 shillings due him
on September 14, 1784.
Court passed an order to be given on the Treasurer to pay
JOHN HOWARD, a disabled soldier, 11 lbs., 10 sh.
Court ordered that the specific articles in the inventory
of EDMUND BULL's estate be equally divided amongst the
representatives of the said EDMUND BULL.
Court approved BENNETT BUSSEY and MARTIN PARKER as security
for EDWARD PARKER, executor of JAMES STEWARD's estate.
ELIZABETH CRETIN applied for a distribution of real estate
of JOHN CRETIN. FREEBORN BROWN and JOHN HAYS, SR. were

18

appointed "to lay of her thirds."

SAMUEL CROSBAY, aged 14 on March 3, 1784, with the consent of his mother, bound to PATRICK FINAGIN until age 21 to learn the cooper's trade and to read, write and cipher as far as the rule of three.

Court released CORNELIOUS CASHMAN from the charge and care of his apprenticed THOMAS DAWSON BANNISTER provided he was bound to a breeches maker and taylor in Baltimore.

OCTOBER COURT, 1784

GEORGE BRADFORD filed a Writ of Error returnable to General Court of this State, but no action could be taken since there was not a sufficient number of Justices to hold a Court. (Only JOHN LOVE and THOMAS BOND were present.)

Citations returnable this term: WILLIAM MORGAN to answer the complaint of DANIEL McCOMAS and wife; ROBERT MORGAN to answer the complaint of SARAH LEWES; JAMES SCOTT (of James) to answer the complaint of ROBERT HARRIS; DANIEL BAYLIS and NATHANIEL BAYLIS to answer the complaint of WILLIAM CULTROUGH; JOHN CAREY to appear in court with JOHN WOOD, orphan of HENRY WOOD; HUGH KIRKPATRICK to answer the complaint of the representatives of ROBERT YOUNG, deceased.

Citations issued for December term: JAMES SCOTT (as above); WILLIAM MORGAN (as above); ROBERT MORGAN (as above); JOHN CAREY (as above); NATHANIEL and DANIEL BAYLIS (as above); SAMUEL BAYLIS to show cause why he had not yet fully settled the estate of SAMUEL BAYLIS, deceased; JAMES BONER and AGNES BONER, late AGNES BAKER, adminx. of NICHOLAS BAKER, deceased, to answer the conplaint of JOHN POGUE; WILLIAM DEBRULAR to answer the complaint of JAMES PRESBURY; WILLIAM ROBINSON and MARY ROBINSON to answer the complaint of WILLIAM JOHNSTON and DAVID JOHNSTON; MICHAEL DIVEN to answer the complaint of JAMES KENNEDY, admin. of ROBERT KENNEDY; THOMAS HALL to show cause why he had not returned an inventory of the goods and chattels of EDWARD VANN of whom he is admin.; BENJAMIN GREEN to answer the complaint of GILES THOMAS.

FEBRUARY COURT, 1785

Justices present: BENEDICT EDWARD HALL, JOHN LOVE, THOMAS BOND, JOHN ARCHER.

Court ordered half pay to disabled soldier JOHN HOWARD for six months from August, 1784.

JESSEE DAVIS, aged 15 on April 20, 1785, bound until age 21 to THOMAS WILSON to learn the cabinet maker's trade and to read, write and cipher as far as the rule of three.

ABRAHAM DAVIS, aged 10 on August 7, 1784, bound to DAVID LEE to learn the miller and cooper's trade, and to learn to read, write and cipher as far as the rule of three.

ROBERT HARRIS agst. JAMES SCOTT (of James). Did not appear.

DANIEL McCOMAS againat WILLIAM MORGAN. Appeared.

SARAH LEWES against ROBERT MORGAN. Did not appear.

JOHN CAREY & JOHN WOOD, orphan of HENRY. Ordered to appear.

SAMUEL BAYLIS, administrator of SAMUEL BAYLIS. Appeared.

WM. COULTROUGH agst.NATHANIEL & DANIEL BAYLIS. Ordered in.

JOHN POGUE against JAMES BONER & AGNES BONER. Appeared.

JAMES PRESBURY against WILLIAM DEBRULER. Ordered to appear.

19

WILLIAM & DAVID JOHNSON agst. WILLIAM & MARY ROBINSON. The
    Court ordered the executors of JOHN COOK to bring in
    and pass their account and then pass a final account.
JAMES KENNEDY against MICHAEL DEVIN. Ordered to appear.
THOMAS HALL appeared and made his return to the Court (with
    respect to good and chattels inventory of EDWARD VANN).
BENJAMIN GREEN ordered to answer complaint of GILES THOMAS.
JAMES JOHNSON, aged 7 on June 28, 1784, bound until age 21
    to JOHN THOMPSON to learn the carpenter's trade, and to
    read, write and cipher as far as the rule of three.
Court ruled that the bonds of JAMES WINEMAN, JAMES VOGAN and
    GEORGE VOGAN respecting a contract for land and a mill
    be cancelled and void by consent of parties concerned.
JOHN KERNS, aged 5 on February 1, 1785, bound until age 21
    to PHILIP MADDEN to learn the weaving trade, and to
    read, write and cypher as far as the rule of three.
JACOB TOLAND, aged 15 on December 9, 1784, bound until age
    21 to JAMES THOMPSON to learn the taylor's trade, and
    to read, write and cipher as far as the rule of three.
SAMUEL WEST, aged 15 on January 18, 1785, bound until age 21
    with the consent of his mother to JAMES MOORES (tanner)
    to learn the tanner's and shoemaker's trade, and to
    "learn him so as to keep his own accounts."
Court admitted the Writ of Error brought by GEORGE BRADFORD
    in a suit brought by WILLIAM RICHARDSON, BENJAMIN
    RICHARDSON, SAMUEL RICHARDSON, JAMES NORRIS and ROBERT
    HAWKINS against the said Bradford. "The Court ordered
    the records and process taken thereon, with all things
    thereunto relating agreeable to the tenor of the said
    Writ of Error, be transmitted under hand and seal to
    General Court of this State the second Tuesday in May."
JOHN ELY, aged 18 on July 6, 1784, bound until age 21 to
    JAMES REARDON to learn the weaver's trade and to learn
    to read, write and cipher as far as the rule of three.

APRIL COURT, 1785
Justices present: JOHN LOVE, THOMAS BOND, WM. SMITH, Esq.
JACOB BILLOW, aged 4 on April 1, 1785, bound until age 21 to
    SAMUEL FORWOOD and his wife SARAH FORWOOD to learn the
    farming business.
SARAH BRYAN, an orphan child aged 7 on July 15, 1784, bound
    until age 16 to JOHN FORWOOD, SR. to learn to read and
    write, and to give her the usual freedoms when age 16.
ROBERT HARRIS agst. JAMES SCOTT (of JAMES): Did not appear.
CHARLES WATERS agst. WILLIAM DEBRULAR & Wife:Did not appear.
SAMUEL CALWELL against EDWARD PARKER: No return.
JAMES KENNEDY against MICHAEL DEVEN: Did not appear.
JOHN POGUE agst. JAMES BONER & AGNESS BONER: Did not appear.
ROBERT MORGAN cited for contempt and to answer the complaint
    of JOHN and SARAH LEWES.
EDWARD BERREY, an orphan child aged 6 years on May 1, 1785,
    bound to WINSTON SMITH to learn to read, write, cipher and
    to learn the farming business, with freedom at 21.
STEPHEN DUTTON (?), a mulatto boy formerly bound to BENJAMIN
    RICHARDSON, who is since deceased, now bound to WINSTON
    SMITH until age 21. Stephen was 15 years old on May 1,
    1785, and he is to learn the farming business.

CHARLES DOE, by consent of his reputed father CHARLES BURKIN who
     states he was 7 years old on December 25, 1784, is bound to
     JACOB BALDERSON and his wife MARY until age 21 to learn the
     farming business or the weaver's trade and to read, write
     and cipher.
WILLIAM LINOM, an orphan aged 14 years on August 1, 1785, is
     bound until age 21 to SAMUEL WEBB, JR. as an apprentice to
     learn the tanners trade and to read, write & cipher.
PATRICK RILEY, aged 14 years on October 1, 1785, bound until age
     21 to SAMUEL WEBB to learn the tanners trade, and to read,
     write and cipher.
EPHRAIM ARNOLD, aged 14 years on September 5, 1785, bound until
     age 21 to JOHN MITCHELL to learn the millwright's trade,
     and to read, write and cipher to the rule of 3.
ADAM EDGCOTH, aged 16 years on October 1, 1784, bound to KIDD
     MORSEL until age 21 to learn the trade of a house carpenter
     and joyner, and to read, write and cipher.
JOHN GOLDSMITH, aged 9 years on October 24, 1785, bound with the
     consent of his mother to JAMES THOMPSON until age 21 to
     learn the taylor's trade and to read, write and cipher to
     the rule of 3.
The court directed the lands of JAMES VAGAN, deceased, be sold
     by his executors for payment of his debts.
On complaint of MICHAEL KELLEY, who was bound by the court to
     JAMES CREITON, said Michael is detained by the court for
     further hearing.
WILLIAM ROBINSON appeared upon summons of WILLIAM JOHNSON and
     DAVID JOHNSON to show cause why he had administered on the
     Estate of JOHN COOK. Court ordered some of the estate to
     be sold to pay debts, and an additional inventory be
     returned on his "land and other things."
Citations ordered by the court: ENOCH WEST to testify about his
     knowledge in a controversy between JAMES CREITON and an
     orphan named MICHAEL KELLEY. WILLIAM GASH and wife to show
     why they had not yet settled the Estate of ROBERT KENNEDY.
     SAMUEL McKISSIN, JOHN BODKIN, GEORGE ANDERSON, WILLIAM
     WILLIAMS, WILLIAM SNODGRASS, and NEHEMIAH BENNINGTON
     summoned (name of case illegible).
THOMAS NORRIS, aged 15 years on May 20, 1785, bound to JOHN
     NORRIS to learn the tanner and currier's trade, and to
     read, write and cipher as far as the rule of three.
The Executors of EDMUND BULL, deacesed, presented an account of
     the inventory which was divided among his heirs as follows:
     The widow's thirds   211 lbs. 14 sh.   3/4 d.
                  RACHEL BULL's share 141 lbs. 2 sh. 8 1/4 d.
                  HESTER BULL's share 141 lbs. 2 sh. 8 1/4 d.
                  MARY BULL's share   141 lbs. 2 sh. 8 1/4 d.
     JAMES CREITON, administrator of RACHEL BULL, ordered to
     distribute a balance of 114 lbs. 14 sh. 1 3/4 p. out of
     specifics in the inventory of the estate of EDMUND BULL
     deceased, in "old Maryland currency dollars," and JAMES
     MOORES and BENNETT MATHEWS were ordered to see it done.
Deposition of WALTER ROBINSON, April 26, 1785, stated that
     SAMUEL HENRY, a little before his death, asked him to draw
     his will, and after giving him the particulars, Robinson
     went home, drew the will with some alteration and carried
     it to Henry, read it to him, and he (Henry) was fully
     satisfied with it and approved it.

Court appointed EDWARD PRAUL, JOSEPH STILES and MAJOR SAMUEL
     SMITH as auditors to settle the Estate of SAMUEL BAYLIS
     deceased.
Court ordered the administrators of BENJAMIN BAYLIS, deceased,
     to make a final statement in the August term.
Court appointed AQUILA SCOTT, EDWARD NORRIS (of Joseph), JOHN
     BOND, JR., and EDWARD NORRIS (of Edward), auditors of the
     Estate of THOMAS RICHARDSON, deceased.
Court made its opinion that the instrument of writing that was
     produced by ISAAC HENRY purporting to be the last will and
     testament of SAMUEL HENRY, is not the will of SAMUEL HENRY,
     and is not to be taken as such.

JUNE COURT, 1785
Justices present: JOHN LOVE, THOMAS BOND, WILLIAM SMITH.
Summoned into Court: SAMUEL McKISSON, NEHEMIAH BENNINGTON,
     GEORGE ANDERSON, JOHN BODKIN, WILLIAM SNODGRASS, AQUILA
     JONES, WILLIAM ARMON, WILLIAM BENNINGTON, MARTHA DUNAN?
     (not legible), AQUILA JONES, JR., AND MARY ANDERSON.
Opinion of the Court respecting SAMUEL HENRY, deceased, was
     continued to the next Court for consideration.
Court summoned JOSEPH ROSE, WILLIAM JONES, JR. and RACHEL NORRIS
     to testify of their knowledge respecting the last will of
     SARAH NORRIS, deceased.
Court ordered that EDWARD CAIN, a maimed soldier with a regular
     discharge, receive annually the sum of eleven pounds and
     five shillings from Harford County at the expiration of
     each year from February, 1783 to 1784.
Court ordered that VALLENTINE SMITH, a maimed soldier, receive
     the sum of seven pounds and ten shillings for six months
     half pay to commence from September 14, 1784 to June 14,
     1785.
Court bound JOHN BULL, aged 16 years on December 1, 1785, with
     the consent of his mother until he reaches age 21, to
     ISSACK BALDERSON to learn the cartwrights trade, wheat fan
     making, and weaving of screens, and give him three months
     schooling.
Court bound WILLIAM DOBBINS, aged 13 years on March 13, 1785
     with the approbation of his father until he reaches age 21,
     to AQUILA NORRIS to learn the shoemakers trade, and to
     read, write and cipher as far as the rule of three.
Court bound PATRICK KELLEY, aged 15 years on October 31, 1784,
     with the consent of his mother until age 21, to PATRICK
     FINNAGAN to learn the coopers trade and to read and write
     and cipher.
Court bound JOHN SCOTT, aged 14 years on May 15, 1785, until he
     reaches age 21, to JAMES WEBSTER (of Jno.) to learn the
     house carpenters and joyners trade, and to read and write
     and cipher as far as the rule of three.
Court bound WILLIAM DUZANS, aged 14 years on April 4, 1785, with
     the consent of his father until he reaches age 21, to JOHN
     HOWARD to learn the taylors trade and receive eight months
     schooling.
Court bound AMOSS OSBORN, aged 19 years on August 10, 1785, with
     his own consent and the consent of his mother, ANN OSBORN,
     until he reaches age 21, to JOHN MITCHELL to learn the
     millwrights trade and get 3 months schooling.
Court bound CHAMBER DINES, aged 17 years on May 15, 1785, to
     JOHN NORRIS, until he reaches age 21 to learn the trade of
     cabinet maker "and to give him no freedoms when he arrives
     to the aforesaid age."

Court bound JOSHUA CHEW, aged 14 years on April 24, 1785, until
he reaches age 21, to DOCTOR JACOB HALL to learn to read,
write and arithmetic "and give him the usual freedom dues
and a horse saddle and bridle when 21."
Court bound GIDEON GILBERT, aged 16 years on May 29, 1785, until
he reaches age 21, to GEORGE VANDERGIFT to learn the
cabinet makers trade "and to give him no freedom dues when
he arrives at the aforesaid age."
Court bound MICHAEL KELLEY (the name "LINDSEY" is written over
top of the surname "KELLEY" in the court record), an orphan
boy being before bound to JAMES CREITON, to AQUILA SCOTT
until 21 to learn the art of agriculture, and to give him
the usual freedoms due at age 21.
Court ordered MORDECAI AMOS, SR., administrator of the goods and
chattels and credits of GEORGE VOGAN, to sell as much
effects as will pay the debts of the deceased.
Court ordered that JOHN LOWREY, a wounded soldier of the 1st
Maryland Regiment and Capt. Adams' Company, who having a
regular discharge which is lost or mislaid, on the
testimony of IGNATIUS WHEELER, JR., Esq., be allowed
fifteen pounds for two years up to June 27, 1785.
Issues brought before the Court: MICHAEL DEVON and JAMES
KENNEDY, administrators of THOMAS KENNEDY, to deliver the
effects of the deceased. WILLIAM MORGAN, executor of
JOSEPH JOHNSON, to finally settle the estate. JOHN COOLEY
to show cause why he misused JAMES WOOD, an orphan boy
bound to him (boy was discharged by the Court). JOSIAS
HITCHCOCK and JOHN LYON to show cause why they had not
fully settled the estate of JONATHAN LYON according to his
will (Court appointed THOMAS HOPE, DANIEL TREDWAY and JOHN
COX as auditors to settle the estate). WILLIAM DEBRULAR and
wife to show cause why they had not settled the estate of
WILLIAM KITELEY according to the Letters of Administration.
The Court appointed securities JOSHUA BROWN and CHARLES
WATERS to take the estate administration into their own
hands and also appointed SAMUEL G. OSBORN and JOSEPH
PRESBURY as their securities. WILLIAM GASH and wife to
show cause why they had not fully settled the estate of
ROBERT KENNEDY according to their Letters of
Administration.
JAMES ROBINSON, WALTER ROBINSON and ELEANOR AKEN to testify for
ISAAC HENRY as to the validity of his fathers will.
DEBORAH LAW to testify in a matter between SKIPWITH JOHNS and
the executors of NATHAN RIGBIE.
JOSEPH PRESBURY, executor of JOSEPH PRESBURY, SR., to answer the
complaint of JAMES PRESBURY as to why he had not complied
with the terms of the last will and testament of JOSEPH
PRESBURY, of which he is executor.

AUGUST COURT, 1785
HOSIER JOHNS, aged 18 years on August 25, 1785, bound until age
21 to DANIEL SHEREDINE to learn his said apprentice the
"morchontile" (mercantile) business.
JOSHUA CUNNINGHAM, an orphan child about the age 10 years, bound
until age 21 to HENRY RUFF to learn the tanners and
curriers trade, and to read, write and cipher as far as the
rule of three.
ELIZABETH BROADERICK, an orphan child formerly bound to JAMES
MATHERS, "his now being dead" the Court binds her to
JOHANNAH MATHERS, widow of the deceased.

HENRY CROSBY, an orphan boy aged 13 years on March 3, 1785, bound with the consent of his mother until age 21 to EDWARD CONN to learn to read, write and cipher as far as the rule of three, with usual freedoms at age 21.

Court ordered JAMES WOOD, an orphan child who was formerly bound to JOHN COOLEY, be released from his master as he is not capable of learning the carpenter's trade.

Court appointed THOMAS HOPE, DANIEL TREDWAY and JOHN COX as auditors to settle the estate of JONATHAN LYON.

Court ordered that negroes Mary, Paraway and Dinah, now in the possession of SKIPWITH JOHNS are to be returned to the Inventory of NATHAN RIGBIE's estate, and that a proportion of the rent of the tract "Rigbie's Hope" shall be returned in said inventory from the time of said Rigbie▮ decease and the 1st of January following.

Court appointed JOHN LOVE, THOMAS JOHNSON, AMBROSE GAUGHOGAN or any two of them as auditors to settle the estates of SAMUEL BAYLIS and BENJAMIN BAYLIS (the above men replacing previously appointed EDWARD PRAUL, JOSEPH STILES, MAJOR SAMUEL SMITH and JAMES CLENDENNING).

MARY PARKER ordered to show cause why she misused MARY JONES (an orphan girl bound to her).

WILLIAM BAKER to answer the complaint of the representatives of JOHN WILSON, deceased.

THOMAS GREENFIELD and wife to show cause why the estates of JAMES KIMBEL and AMASA TAYLOR are not fully settled.

JOHN FORWOOD and SAMUEL FORWOOD to answer the complaint of the administrator of JOSEPH FORWOOD.

OCTOBER COURT, 1785, ADJOURNED TO NOVEMBER, 1785

JOHN THOMAS to answer the complaint of THOMAS STEEL as to why the estate of DAVID THOMAS was not fully settled.

MARY PARKER to answer the complaint of SARAH DEAVON.

MARY COX and WILLIAM COX, executors of WILLIAM COX, to answer the complaint of JOHN COX about the selling (or settling?) of the estate of the deceased, WILLIAM COX.

SARAH HILL, executrix of AARON HILL, to answer the complaint of JAMES HILL.

THOMAS GREENFIELD and wife to answer the complaint of ROBERT TAYLOR and show cause why the estates of JAMES KIMBEL and AMASA TAYLOR were not fully settled.

THOMAS CHISHOLM and MARY BALEY to testify the truth of their knowledge respecting SAMUEL McCARTIE's last will.

STEPHEN TAYLOR to testify the truth of his knowledge respecting SAMUEL McCARTIE's last will.

CATHARINE ANDERSON to answer the complaint of CHARLES BUCKINGHAM.

MARY SIMS to answer the complaint of ANTHONY LINCH.

RICHARD WILMOTT to answer the complaint of ANTHONY LINCH.

JOHN MOORE and wife to show cause why they had not fully settled the estate of ROBERT BROWN according to their Letters of Administration.

FEBRUARY COURT, 1786, ADJOURNED TO MARCH, 1786

MATHEW CONKLIN to answer the complaint of THOMAS GASH and LAWRENCE CLARK.

JOHN THOMAS to answer the complaint of THOMAS STEEL.

APRIL COURT, 1786

THOMAS GREENFIELD and wife to answer the complaint of ROBERT
TAYLOR as to why the estate of AMASA TAYLOR had not been
fully settled.

JAMES BONER and wife to answer the complaint of JOHN POGUE.

JAMES MITCHELL to answer the complaint of SARAH MITCHELL.

RACHEL KILLISCORE, aged 5 years on March 18, 1785 (1786?), bound
until age 16 to JOHN INGRAM and SARAH, his wife, to learn
to sew, knit and receive one year's schooling.

JAMES CREWS, aged 6 years on October 1, 1786 (1785?), bound to
MICHAEL DENNEY until age 21 to learn the business of
farming, and read, write and cipher to the rule of 3.

THOMAS HAYSE (HAYES?), an orphan child aged 12 years on February
15, 1786, bound until age 21 to JAMES MOORE, JR. to learn
the shoemakers trade or craft, and to read, write and
cipher to the rule of three.

JOHN HOSHEA, aged 16 years on April 12, 1786, bound until age 21
to CATHARINE McLOUGHLIN to learn to read, write and cipher
to the rule of 3, with usual freedoms at 21.

ABRAHAM AIRS, aged 11 years on September 15, 1785, bound until
age 21 to JOHN KIMBALL to learn to read, write, cipher to
the rule of 3, with usual freedoms at age 21.

Court ordered testimony by ISAAC HENRY on the estate of SAMUEL
HENRY.

STOCKETT OGG, who was bound to MATTHEW DORSEY to learn a trade,
is to also receive one year's schooling.

JOSHUA ARMSTRONG, aged 16 years on November 3, 1785, bound until
age 21 to GEORGE TAYLOR to learn the shoemaker's craft or
trade, and to receive three year's schooling.

THOMAS MAXWELL, aged 17 years on January 28, 1786, bound until
age 21 to CUTHBERT WARNER to learn the watchmaker trade,
and read, write and cipher to the rule of three.

THOMAS ARMSTRONG, aged 12 years in May, 1785, bound with the
consent of his mother until age 21 to MATTHEW SNOWDAY to
learn the carpenter's trade, and read, write and cipher as
far as the rule of three.

CORBIN LEE, son of JAMES LEE, deceased, came into Court and
chose SAMUEL WILSON his guardian, and offered ALEXANDER
COWAN and JOHN TAYLOR as securities. Court approved.

Court bound NEGRO LUKE, aged 15 years on April 12, 1786, to
SKIPWITH JOHNS, with the usual freedoms at age 21.

Court appointed DR. JOHN ARCHER, JOHN WILSON (merchant) and
JOSEPH MILLER (fuller) as auditors to settle the accounts
of COL. NATHAN RIGBIE and NATHAN RIGBIE, JR.

JEMINA ROBINSON, aged 7 years on November 15, 1786, bound until
age 16 to SIMON MESSHEL to learn to read and write, and to
receive the usual freedoms at age 16.

EDWARD LEE, aged 14 years on March 15, 1786, bound until age 21
to WILLIAM COALE to learn to read, write and cipher as far
as the rule of 3, with usual freedoms at age 21.

LAWSON McKEYE, aged 4 years on April 1, 1786, bound until age 21
to JOHN BARNHOUSE to learn the shoemaker's trade and to
read, write and cipher as far as the rule of 3.

JAMES WOOD, aged 17 years and 3 months on April 13, 1786, bound
until age 21 to JOHN WILSON to learn the taylor's trade and
to receive 6 months' schooling.

WILLIAM McKENLEY, aged 12 years on April 13, 1786, bound to JOHN
DEMOSS until age 21 and to receive two year's schooling and

at the expiration of this time to give him one horse, ten pounds
    specie, one saddle and bridle and a suit of good cloaths
    when he arrives at age 21.
WILLIAM JOHNSON, executor, and MARY ROBINSON, executrix, of the
    last will and testament of JOHN COOK, ordered by the Court
    to fully settle the estate and make a return.
Court appointed DANIEL TREDWAY and JOHN COX as auditors to
    settle the estate of BENJAMIN RICHARDSON between the
    executor of his will and WILLIAM RICHARDSON.

MAY COURT, 1786
JOHN HOWARD, a maimed soldier of Col. Nichola's Corps of
    Invalids, is allowed his whole due up to Feb., 1786.
VALENTINE SMITH, a maimed soldier of Col. Nichola's Corps of
    Invalids, is allowed 11 lbs. 5 sh. up to June 14, 1786.
EDWARD CAIN, a maimed soldier of the 4th Maryland Regiment, is
    allowed 11 lbs. 5 sh. up to June 14, 1786.
Letters of Administration granted to THOMAS MILES on the estate
    of JOHN MILES, deceased, he being next of kin and heir at
    law to the deceased, with WILLIAM SMITH, ESQ. and THOMAS
    STREET approved as securities.

JUNE COURT, 1786
JOHN THOMAS, administrator of DAVID THOMAS, to answer the
    complaint of THOMAS STEEL.
ELIZABETH CREIGH, JOHN LOVE and ROBERT HARRIS to answer the
    complaint of MARK McGOVERNG.
MARY DINES to show cause why she had not fully administered the
    estate of FRANCIS DINES.
SAMUEL WEBB, JR. to answer the complaint of ROBERT HARRIS.
THOMAS GREENFIELD and wife to answer the complaint of REBECCA
    PIKE, and the complaint of ROBERT TAYLOR.
MATTHEW CONKLIN and wife to answer the complaint of THOMAS GASH
    and LAWRENCE CLARK.
THOMAS MITCHELL came into Court and chose GABRIEL MITCHELL as
    his guardian.
Court bound THOMAS MITCHELL, aged 14 years on September 22,
    1785, to GABRIEL MITCHELL until age 21 to learn the
    millwright's trade and to read, write and cipher as far as
    the rule of 3, with the usual freedoms at age 21.
Court ordered JAMES MITCHELL to deliver into the possession of
    GABRIEL MITCHELL, all the estate devised by WILLIAM
    MITCHELL, deceased, to THOMAS MITCHELL, as his chosen
    guardian to the said THOMAS MITCHELL agreeable to law.
Court approved JOHN MITCHELL and JOSEPH ROLES as securities for
    the estate of THOMAS MITCHELL.
JAMES HART, aged 10 years on March 25, 1786, bound until age 21
    with the consent of his mother to GEDION PERVALE to learn
    the joyner's trade and to read, write and cipher as far as
    the rule of 3, with the usual freedoms at 21.
RALPH PILES, SR. appointed guardian of SARAH THOMAS, age 12,
    HANNAH THOMAS, age 8, and ANNA THOMAS, age 4, all being
    children of HENRY THOMAS, JR., deceased.
HENRY GREEN and BENJAMIN GREEN appointed to go with the
    Commissioners of the County to estimate the annual value of
    the lands of HENRY THOMAS, JR., deceased.
Court appointed SAMUEL HUGHS, Esq. and WILLIAM SMITH, Esq.,
    (Bayside) as auditors to settle accounts between JAMES

BONER and AGNES BONER, administrators of NICHOLAS BAKER
JR., deceased. JOHN POGUE to report same to the Court.
FRANCIS GREEN, aged 14 years on March 7, 1786, bound with the
consent of his uncle HENRY GREEN to JOHN GRENDALL until age
21 to learn the taylor's trade and to read, write and
cipher as far as the rule of three.
Court ordered the accounts between MARTHA NORRIS (on account of
JOHN NORRIS, deceased) and WILLIAM McCOMAS (executor of
DANIEL McCOMAS, deceased) be audited and settled by JAMES
SINCLEAR and JOHN COX to credit of WM. McCOMAS.
RACHEL SWIFT, aged 13 years on September 15, 1786, bound until
age 16 to MARGARET SCARBOROUGH to learn the Bible and to
receive a linsey jackett, petticoat, two shifts and a pair
of shoes when she reaches age 16.
JAMES ANDERSON, aged 12 years on February 1, 1787, bound to JOHN
RENSHAW until age 21 to learn the shoemakers trade and to
read, write and cipher as far as the rule of 3.

AUGUST COURT, 1786
Citations issued by the Court for these appearances: STEPHEN
HILL and JAMES RIGDON to answer the complaint of MARY
VANCLEAVE. MARY PARKER to bring MARY JONES, an orphan
bound to her, to Court to answer misuse charges. THOMAS
GREENFIELD & FRANCES GREENFIELD to answer the complaint of
REBECCA PIKE. THOMAS GREENFIELD & FRANCES GREENFIELD to
also answer the complaint of ROBERT TAYLOR.
DAVID HAMPTON, age 9 years on September 17, 1786, bound with the
consent of his mother to JOHN CUMINGS and his wife until
age 21 to learn the farming business, and to give him three
year's schooling, and the usual freedom dues when 21, "that
is to say, a good suit of cloaths and a suit of working
cloaths, etc."
WILLIAM HUGINS, age 5 years on March 7, 1786, bound with the
consent of his parents to THOMAS SAMPSON until age 21 to
learn the weaver trade and to read, write and cipher as far
as the rule of 3, with usual freedoms at age 21.
Commissioners present in Court, August 21, 1786: JOHN LOVE,
THOMAS BOND, WILLIAM SMITH, and WILLIAM SMITHSON.
Court granted Letter of Administration to WILLIAM RICHARDSON on
the Estate of SAMUEL CURREY. Securities approved by the
Court: BENJAMIN B. NORRIS, WILLIAM ROBINSON, and JOHN
BARROW. Letters sent to the Court at its request by WILLIAM
BRADFORD. Signed by J. GEO. BRADFORD.
Court appointed JOHN COX and DANIEL TREDWAY as auditors to
settle the accounts between the legatees of BENJAMIN
RICHARDSON, deceased, and the heirs of ELIZABETH DAVIS, and
to settle the accounts between WILLIAM RICHARDSON and the
executor of the last will and testament of BENJAMIN
RICHARDSON and to report at the October Court.
Citations issued: JAMES CRETIN to answer the complaint of
ELIZABETH CRETIN. ALEX. RIGDON to answer complaint of
THOMAS MILES, administrator of JOHN MILES, deceased.
JOHN COX and WILLIAM COX, executors of WILLIAM COX, dec'd.,
appeared in consequence of a citation prayed by JOHN COX in
December, 1785, to show cause why they had not fully
settled the Estate of WILLIAM COX, deceased. WILLIAM COX
gave the following reason: JOHN COX was in possession of a
mill and twenty acres of land which he (WILLIAM COX)
apprehended was part of said estate, and with this in

27

dispute, the estate had not been settled. The Court
determined that the mill and land of JOHN COX was not a
part of the estate of WILLIAM COX, deceased.
Court appointed JOHN WILSON (merchant), DR. JOHN ARCHER, and
DANIEL SHERIDINE to audit and settle the accounts of JOHN
COX and the Estate of WILLIAM COX, deceased.
Citations issued by Court: JAMES CRETIN to answer complaint of
ELIZABETH CRETIN. JAMES KIDD to answer complaint of ROBERT
DUNWOOD and wife. SAMUEL WEBB, JR. to answer complaint of
ROBERT HARRIS. STEPHEN HILL and JAMES RIGDON to answer
complaint of MARY VANCLEAVE. JAMES DERNEY to answer
complaint of ROBERT SCOTT and BENJAMIN FORD. MATTHEW
CONKLING and wife to answer complaint of THOMAS GASH and
LAWRENCE CLARK. BENNETT JARRETT to answer complaint of
WILLIAM RICHARDSON, administrator of SAMUEL CURRY.
ALEXANDER RIGDON to answer complaint of THOMAS MILES,
administrator of JOHN MILES.
NATHAN SHERIDINE, son and heir of JEREMIAH SHERIDINE and
CASSANDRA SHERIDINE, legatees of NATHAN RIGBIE, chose UPTON
SHERIDINE of Frederick County as his guardian. UPTON
SHERIDINE appeared and offered as his securities, BAZEL
DORSEY, EPHRAIM HOWARD and DANIEL DORSEY (all of Frederick
County) and they were approved by the Court.
Court granted to VALLENTINE SMITH (a maimed soldier) that an
allowance be made up to him in the amount of 15 pounds,
including 11 pounds, 5 shillings he already received.
ELIZABETH JONES, age 9 years on March 14, 1786, bound until age
16 to MARY PIKE to learn to read the Bible and to write a
fair hand, with the usual freedoms at age 16.
Court ordered MARY PARKER to give up MARY JONES (who was bound
to her by the Court) to her mother SARAH DEACON (DEAVON?),
and to show cause why she misused her.
Citations issued: THOMAS GREENFIELD and wife to answer
complaint of REBECCA PIKE. MARY PARKER to show cause why
she misused MARY JONES, an orphan, bound to her.
THOMAS BROOKS, age 14 years on January 1, 1787, bound until age
21 to CHARLES BUSKIN to learn the nailmakers trade and to
read, write and cipher as far as the rule of 3.
WILLIAM WOODLAND DORNEY, age 10 years on March 30, 1786, bound
until age 21 to ALEXANDER COWAN to learn to read, write and
cipher as far as the rule of three.
ANDREW NEVIN, in Court, chose THOMAS HOPE as his guardian.
VINSON GOLDSMITH, age 7 years on April 10, 1786, bound with the
consent of his mother to BARNARD PRESTON until age 21 to
learn the farming business and to read, write and cipher as
far as the rule of three.
Court ordered the administratrix of JOHN CREIGHTEN, dec'd., to
pay ELIZABETH ANN HARDY ("otherwise ELIZABETH ANN
McSHERRY"), her part of said estate with interest from the
time she arrived at the age of 16 years.
Court ordered WILLIAM ROBINSON & wife to give up the Estate of
JOHN COOK, deceased, to WILLIAM JOHNSON, one of the
executors of the last will and testament of JOHN COOK,
deceased, who will complete the estate administration.
JOHN COYLE, a maimed soldier of the 1st Maryland Regiment, was
granted 7 pounds, 10 sh., up to June 27, 1786, and two
orders (1787) given for 5 lbs. and 2 lbs. 10 sh.

28

DECEMBER COURT, 1786
Court Justices present: WILLIAM SMITH and WILLIAM SMITHSON.
Court adjourned until February, 1787, with the following
    citation being issued: STEPHEN TAYLOR and ABRAHAM TAYLOR
    to answer complaint of SAMUEL BEARD. ELIJAH BLACKSTON to
    show cause why he had not fully settled the Estate of
    EDWARD GARRETSON and to answer complaint of JOHN LEE
    WEBSTER. JOSEPH LUSBY to show cause why he had not fully
    settled the Estate of BETTEY LUSBY and to also answer the
    complaint of JOHN LEE WEBSTER. THOMAS GREENFIELD & wife to
    answer complaint of REBECCA PIKE.

FEBRUARY COURT, 1787
JOHN CRAWFORD, age 16 years on July 15, 1786, bound until age 21
    to JAMES WALKER to learn the tanner and curriers trade,
    with the usual freedoms at age 21.
Court ordered COL. ALEX. RIGDON to deliver up all papers and
    accounts related to the Estate of JANE MILES, deceased, to
    THOMAS MILES, administrator of the goods & chattels of JOHN
    MILES, and that said administrator pay all just debts of
    JANE MILES and COL. ALEX. RIGDON's account.
Court ordered that the Estate of WILLIAM AMOSS, deceased, be
    accountable to the Estate of JOSHUA AMOSS, deceased, in the
    sum of 247 lbs. 14 sh. 2 d. as it was in Sept.1779.
WILLIAM WOOLLING, age 12 years on February 17, 1787, bound until
    21 to ROBERT CONN to learn the farming business, and to
    read, write and cipher as far as the rule of 3.
LEONARD WOOLLING, age 10 years on June 10, 1787, bound until age
    21 to JOSEPH BAY to learn the farming business, and to
    read, write and cipher as far as the rule of 3.
WILLIAM HILL, age 14 years (birth date not stated) bound until
    age 21 to DAVID HORRY to learn the coopers trade, and to
    read, write and cipher as far as the rule of 3.
Court ordered the Letters of Administration on the Estate of
    JOHN DORNEY, deceased, be revoked and Letters De Bonis Non
    be granted to ROBERT SCOTT and BENJAMIN FORD, the
    securities of the former administrator of the estate.
Court ordered the Letters of Administration on the Estate of
    EDWARD ROBINSON, deceased, be revoked and Letters De Bonis
    Non be granted to JAMES TAYLOR upon his giving good
    security.
Court appointed THOMAS HOPE as guardian to ANDREW NEVIN and
    approved DANIEL TREDWAY and PATRICK COWAN, securities.
JAMES SCOTT, a maimed soldier of the 1st Maryland Regiment, was
    granted 7 pounds, 10 sh. for one year's support.
JOHN HOWARD, a maimed soldier of Col. Nichola's Corps of
    Invalids, was granted 10 pounds up to February, 1787.

APRIL COURT, 1787
Court Justices: JOHN LOVE, THOMAS BOND, WILLIAM SMITHSON.
WILLIAM HOLLIS, administrator of WILLIAM HOLLIS, deceased, to
    show cause why he had not returned an inventory of the
    goods and chattels of the deceased, and to answer the
    complaint of JESSE BUSSEY. The Court was divided on this
    matter, so an appeal was prayed for a removal of the case
    to the General Court, and it was signed.
CATHARINE ANDERSON to answer complaint of JAMES MOORE and wife.
    She did not appear, so an attachment was issued.

BENNETT JARRETT to answer complaint of WILLIAM RICHARDSON. Court summoned HENRY RICHARDSON, ISSACH MOFFITT, and MORDECAI AMOSS (of James). All appeared. The Court appointed JOHN TAYLOR and RICHARD BIDDLE as auditors to settle the matter and to return an award to the Court.

Court appointed DANIEL TREDWAY and THOMAS HOPE to divide the lands, late the property of JOHN KIDD, according to the "terms and effects of his will between his sons, as the representatives of one of them who is deceased and the son surviving."

Attachment ordered for CATHARINE ANDRESON for contempt and to answer the complaint of JAMES MOORE and wife. All appeared and Court ordered CATHARINE ANDERSON to pay unto CHARLES BUCKINGHAM "twenty one lbs., nineteen sh. and one penney half penney with nine year's interest."

SAMUEL LEE to answer complaint of BARNARD PRESTON. Lee did not appear, so an attachment was issued.

ABRAHAM TAYLOR and SOLOMON ARMSTRONG to answer complaint of BENJAMIN EVERIST. EDWARD THOMPSON summoned in behalf of the plaintiff. All appeared and the Court ordered that ABRAHAM TAYLOR will keep the negro given to him and his wife by her father, THOMAS EVERIST, and SOLOMON ARMSTRONG will keep the negro given to his wife and him by her father, THOMAS EVERIST.

THOMAS GREENFIELD and wife to answer complaint of JAMES TAYLOR. All appeared, but no disposition of case cited.

AMOS HOLLIS to answer complaint of WILLIAM HOLLIS. Appeared in Court, but no disposition of case cited.

HANNAH COOP to answer complaint of MOSES JOHNSON. Appeared in Court, but no disposition of case cited.

ALEXANDER RIGDON, administrator of BARNABY CONNOLLY, to show cause why the estate had not been fully settled, and to answer complaint of JAMES LEONARD. HUGH WHITEFORD was summoned for the plaintiff. (No disposition cited.)

Court released JAMES WALKER from any engagement he was under to learn LUKE HANSON the tanner and curriers trade.

Court appointed ROBERT AMOSS and WILLIAM SMITH, Esq., as auditors to settle the accounts of ABRAHAM WHITAKER and ALEXANDER CRAWFORD, both deceased.

Court ordered the Estate of JOHN COOK out of the hands of the former administrators and Letters De Bonis Non be granted to WILLIAM JOHNSON.

JUNE COURT, 1787
Court Justices: BENEDICT EDWARD HALL, JOHN LOVE, WILLIAM SMITH, and WILLIAM SMITHSON.

JOSHUA WOOD came to Court and chose AMOSS BARNES as his guardian. BENJAMIN OSBORN and JACOB GREENFIELD were approved as securities.

Court ordered Letters De Bonis Non be granted to JAMES WEBSTER on the Estate of JOHN MOORE, deceased.

Court ordered Letters De Bonis Non be granted to ABRAHAM TAYLOR on the Estate of JAMES KIMBAL, deceased.

DANIEL SCOTT, administrator of the goods, chattels and credits of WILLIAM COALE, deceased, prayed the Court for guidance on disposing of a leasehold and patented property of the deceased. Court ordered DANIEL SCOTT to dispose of the leasehold and certificate estate as other chattels, and likewise for the lot in Belle Air.

30

AUGUST COURT, 1787

ISAAC MILES came into Court and chose THOMAS MILES as his
    guardian, with HENRY RICHARDSON and JOHN WATKINS as
    securities.
JAMES MILES came into Court and chose THOMAS MILES as his
    guardian (same securities as ISAAC MILES above).
Court granted JOHN LOWREY, a maimed soldier of the First
    Maryland Regiment, half pay of 7 pounds, 10 shillings, up
    to June 27, 1787. Order given to IGNATIUS WHEELER, Esq.,
    on August 14, 1787.
HANNAH COOP to answer complaint of MOSES JOHNSON, appeared in
    Court and was ordered to deliver to MOSES JOHNSON,
    administrator of RICHARD COOP, one feather bed and colt and
    cow, the late property of RICHARD COOP.
BENJAMIN ANDERSON and SARAH ANDERSON to answer complaint of
    WILLIAM SLADE. Appeared.
MARY CONNELLEY to answer complaint of ALEXANDER RIGDON, appeared
    and the Court revoked the Letters of Administration on the
    Estate of BARNEBY CONNELLEY and granted Letters De Bonis
    Non to ALEXANDER RIGDON. Also, the surviving appraiser of
    BARNEBY CONNELLEY's estate gave an amended report on the
    November 1777 appraisal.

OCTOBER COURT, 1787

Court Justices: JOHN LOVE, THOMAS BOND, WILLIAM SMITHSON, and
    WILLIAM SMITH.
WILLIAM COLTROUGH to answer complaint about his guardianship of
    orphans SAMUEL BAYLIS and BENJAMIN BAYLIS. Appeared and the
    case was dismissed since he was in compliance.
BENNETT MATHEWS to answer complaint about his guardianship of
    orphan ANN MATHEWS. Appeared and case was dismissed.
JOHN DAY to answer complaint about his guardianship of LEVEN
    MATHEWS and ELIZABETH FILLISANNE MATHEWS, orphans. The
    record stated he "did not appear due to being sick."
JAMES THOMPSON to answer complaint about his guardianship of
    orphans DAVIS McCRACKING and ELIZABETH McCRACKING. He
    appeared and case was dismissed due to his compliance.
WILLIAM BAKER to answer complaint about his guardianship of
    orphans JAMES WILSON, BENJAMIN WILSON and AVARILLA WILSON.
    He did not appear (no reason stated).
EDWARD BEVEN to answer complaint about his guardianship of
    orphan LEONARD GREEN. He did not appear (no reason).
RALPH PYLE to answer complaint about his guardianship of orphans
    SARAH THOMAS, HANNAH THOMAS and ANNA THOMAS, appeared and
    ordered to comply with Act of Assembly; posted bond.
    Securities: JOHN LOVE & IGNATIUS WHEELER.
GABRIEL MITCHELL to answer complaint about his guardianship of
    THOMAS MITCHELL, orphan.   (Nothing recorded)
GARRETT GARRETSON to answer complaint about his guardianship of
    BENJAMIN GARRETSON and JAMES GARRETSON. Appeared. "JAMES
    GARRETSON paid off; BENJAMIN dead."
THOMAS BUCKINGHAM to answer complaint about his guardianship of
    ZACHARIAH AMOS and ELIJAH AMOS, orphans. (No return)
JOHN LONG, JR. to answer complaint about his guardianship of
    CASSANDRA SCOTT, orphan. Appeared and case dismissed by his
    complying with the several acts of assembly in that case,
    and paying fees.
ANN BRIERLY to answer complaint about her guardianship of THOMAS
    BRIERLY, orphan. Appeared (nothing recorded).

31

SAMUEL GRAFTON to answer complaint about his guardianship of
WILLIAM McGOVEREN, orphan. Did not appear.
PHILIP COALE to answer complaint of JAMES GILES (no return).
THOMAS GILES to answer complaint of JAMES GILES (no return).
STEPHEN HILL and JAMES RIGDON to answer complaint of MARTHA
SMITH. Appeared (nothing recorded).
JAMES RILEY to answer complaint of ROBERT FORSTER. Appeared.
Ordered by the Court to settle Estate of BARNEY RILEY.
SAMUEL WEBSTER, RICHARD WEBSTER & MICHAEL WEBSTER to answer
complaint of JAMES RENSHAW. Appeared (nothing recorded)
WILLIAM HITCHCOCK to answer complaint about his guardianship of
SAMSON EGAN, MARY EGAN, CLEMENTINE EGAN, and SARAH EGAN.
Appeared and case dismissed due to his complying.
WILLIAM JOHNSON to answer complaint of FRANCES GORDON. Appeared
(nothing recorded).
Court ordered JAMES RILEY, acting executor of BARNEY RILEY, to
settle up fully & pass a final account by Oct. 23rd.
EDWARD CAIN, a maimed soldier of the 4th Maryland Regiment, of
Colonel Hall, granted 11 pounds, 5 shillings.
VALLENTINE SMITH, a maimed soldier of Col. Nichola's Corps of
Invalids, granted 15 pounds up to September 14th.
JOSIAS JOHNSON came into Court and chose DAVID CLARK as his
guardian. Securities: THOMAS JOHNSON & BARNETT JOHNSON.
JAMES CREITON to answer complaint of ELIZABETH CREITON.
MARY VANCLEAVE to answer complaint of MARTHA SMITH and show
cause why JOHN VANCLEAVE's estate had not been settled.
MARY FLANNAGAN to answer the complaint of DR. FRANCIS NEAL.
ALEXANDER RIGDON and ANN RIGDON, executrix of the goods and
chattels of JOHN JOHNSON, deceased, to show cause why the
estate of the deceased had not been fully settled. Both
appeared. "Matters settled so far."
WILLIAM HOLLIS to show cause why the estate of WILLIAM HOLLIS,
deceased, had not been fully settled, and to answer
complaint of JESSE BUSSEY.
Court appointed WILLIAM BRADFORD & JOHN McCOMAS (of Daniel) to
appraise the goods and chattels of........ WALTHOM paid
into the hands of JOHN HUSTON, late of Harford County,
dec'd., and now in the hands of ROBERT DUTTON, executor of
the deceased's last will and testament.

FEBRUARY COURT, 1788
By rule of the Orphans Court in the April Term of 1787 in a case
involving WILLIAM RICHARDSON, the administrator of SAMUEL
CURRY, deceased (plaintiff) and BENNETT JARRETT
(defendant), arbitrators JOHN TAYLOR and RICHARD BIDDLE
considered the allegations and examined the witnesses and
evidence, and have determined that BENNETT JARRETT shall
pay unto WILLIAM RICHARDSON the sum of 5 pounds, 15
shillings, and the cost of this suit, and give up the
co-partnership book of said CURRY & JARRETT to said
Richardson and all accounts the said Jarrett may have in
his possession relative to the partnership. Given under
their hands this 7th day of February, 1788.
JAMES CREITON to answer the complaint of ELIZABETH CREITON.
SAMUEL WEBSTER (of Samuel), RICHARD WEBSTER, MICHAEL WEBSTER and
JOHN BARNEY to testify on their knowledge of a matter
pending between JAMES RENSHAW and the estate of SAMUEL
WEBSTER, deceased. Appeared.

ELIZABETH CREIGH, JOHN LOVE, Esq., and ROBERT HARRIS, executors of ABRAHAM WHITAKER, deceased, to show cause why they had not fully settled the estate. Appeared.

WILLIAM HOLLIS, administrator of WILLIAM HOLLIS, deceased, to show cause why he had not fully settled the estate and also to answer the complaint of JESSE BUSSEY.

SAMUEL WEBB to answer the complaint of ROBERT HARRIS.

KENT MITCHELL to answer the complaint of MICAJAH MITCHELL.

SAMUEL SMITH (of Robert), MARY SMITH, and LILE SMITH to answer the complaint of WILLIAM SMITH (of Robert).

MARCH COURT, 1788
SAMUEL GRIFFITH to show cause why he had not fully settled the estate of GEORGE GARRETSON and to give an account of his guardianship to the orphans of said Garretson.

WILLIAM HOLLIS, administrator of WILLIAM HOLLIS, deceased, to show cause why he had not passed a final account on his administration and answer JESSE BUSSEY's complaint.

WILLIAM HOPKINS and ELIZABETH HUSBANDS to answer complaint of JOSHUA HUSBANDS.

JOSEPH DYER to answer complaint of HENRY RUFF. Summons issued for JAMES BENNETT to testify for the plaintiff.

SAMUEL SMITH, MARY SMITH (his wife) and LILE SMITH to answer complaint of WILLIAM SMITH (of Robert).

JAMES CREITON to answer the complaint of ELIZABETH CREITON.

MARY FLANNAGAN to answer the complaint of DR. FRANCIS NEAL.

GEORGE YOUNG to answer complaint of WILLIAM WILSON (of Wm.).

APRIL COURT, 1788
JACOB MAXWELL to answer the complaint of CORBIN COULTER.

JOSEPH DYER to answer complaint of HENRY RUFF. Summoned JAMES BENNETT to testify for the plaintiff.

ROBERT SCOTT and BENJAMIN FORD, Administrators De Bonis Non of the goods and chattels of JOHN DORNEY, deceased, to answer complaint of WILLIAM MORRIS, a representative.

SAMUEL CUMMINS and SARAH CUMMINS (COMMINS) to answer the complaint of REBECCA CALHOON, admx. of MARY HARE.

JUNE COURT, 1788
Justices: BENEDICT EDWARD HALL, JOHN LOVE, WILLIAM SMITHSON.

Court appointed JOHN McNABB and THOMAS JOHNSON, Esq., to audit and settle the estate of BENJAMIN WHEELER, late of Harford County. (Conditions placed by the Court on the audit indicated that BENJAMIN WHEELER left a widow)

Court appointed HENRY WILSON, DR. JOHN ARCHER and JOHN COX to audit the accounts of WILLIAM HUSBANDS and JOSEPH HUSBANDS who both were deceased. (Note entered into the record in 1791 indicated that the Court "reappointed JOHN LEE GIBSON and JOHN COX for the above purpose.")

SAMUEL LEE, administrator of GEDION VANCLEAVE, to show cause why he had not fully settled the estate, and to answer the complaint of BARNARD PRESTON.

Court appointed THOMAS GIBSON, SAMUEL RAIN, and JAMES CLENDENNIN to audit the accounts of CAPT. ROBERT HARRIS and the Acting Executors of ABRAHAM WHITAKER, deceased, accounts against said Whitaker's estate.

Letters of Administration that had been granted to REBECCA
    CALHOON on the goods and chattels of MARY HARE were revoked
    by the Court and then granted to JAMES HARE.
Court appointed WILLIAM SMITH (Bayside), GREENBERRY DORSEY, JOHN
    LEE WEBSTER, JOSIAS WILLIAM DALLAM and SAMUEL HUGHES, Esq.,
    to settle all matters in dispute between the administrators
    and representatives of the estate of GEORGE GARRETSON, late
    of Harford County.
JOHN BARTON BIDDLE came into Court and chose RICHARD BIDDLE as
    his guardian. JAMES BARTON and ABRAHAM JARRETT were
    approved as securities.
Court appointed RICHARD BIDDLE guardian of RICHARD BIDDLE (of
    Benjamin). JAMES BARTON & ABRAHAM JARRETT were approved as
    securities.
ELISHA JARRETT, aged 14 years, came into Court and chose ABRAHAM
    JARRETT as his guardian. RICHARD BIDDLE and BENJAMIN
    PRESTON were approved as securities.
Court allowed JOHN HOWARD, a maimed soldier of Col.Nichola's
    Corps of Invalids, 7 pounds, 10 sh., up to Feb., 1788.
Court allowed EDWARD CAIN, a maimed soldier of 4th Maryland
    Regiment, 11 pounds, 5 shillings, up to June 19, 1788.
Court allowed VALLENTINE SMITH, a maimed soldier of Colonel
    Nichola's Corps of Invalids, 15 pounds for one year's
    support, up to September 14, 1788.
Court allowed JAMES SCOTT, a maimed soldier of 1st Maryland
    Regiment, 7 pounds, 10 shillings for one year's support up
    to February, 1788.

AUGUST COURT, 1788
Justices: JOHN LOVE, WILLIAM SMITHSON, and WILLIAM SMITH.
SAMUEL LEE ordered to finally settle the estate of DOCTOR GIDEON
    VANCLEAVE of which he is administrator.
WILLIAM HOLLIS, administrator of WILLIAM HOLLIS, deceased, to
    show cause why he had not fully settled the estate. He
    appeared in Court and "the matter was postponed to the
    October Court by informing the Court that his father's
    estate is blended with his grandfather's estate and that
    with the Estate of WILLIAM SNELSON."
BLOYCE WRIGHT came into Court and chose THOMAS WRIGHT as his
    guardian. JAMES SCIVINGTON and EDWARD FLANNAGAN were
    approved as securities.
JOHN WRIGHT came into Court and chose MATTHEW SPARKS as his
    guardian. JAMES SCIVINGTON and EDWARD FLANNAGAN were
    approved as securities.
Court appointed THOMAS WRIGHT as guardian to WILLIAM WRIGHT.
    Securities were JAMES SCIVINGTON and EDWARD FLANNAGAN.
Court ordered that the will, or office copy of the will, of
    BENJAMIN WHEELER, late of Harford County then Baltimore
    County, and other such estate papers, be recorded.

OCTOBER COURT, 1788
Court ruled that the two bonds due from HENRY D. GOUGH and
    GEORGE BUCHANAN to ELIZABETH HOWARD, now the wife of JESSE
    BUSSEY, be struck out of the List of Separate Debts of
    WILLIAM HOLLIS, deceased, her former busband.
SAMUEL WEBB, administrator of WILLIAM WEBB, late of Harford
    County, to show cause why he had returned an inventory of

the goods and chattels of the deceased and to answer the
complaint of ROBERT HARRIS & IGNATIUS WHEELER, Esq.
MARY FORWOOD came into Court and chose SAMUEL FORWOOD as her
guardian. Securities: BARNARD PRESTON and JAMES HOLMES.
ABRAHAM WHITAKER's assumption to JAMES HONER of 55 pounds, 5
shillings, payable at November Court, 1780 and notice to be
given to McCREIGH (no first name given) to show what
payments have been made, before January 1, 1789.
THOMAS GIBSON, JAMES CLENDENING and SAMUEL RAINE having been
appointed by the Court to settle the account between the
executors of ABRAHAM WHITAKER, deceased, and ROBERT HARRIS,
determined that the estate of said Whitaker is bonafide
indebted unto said Harris in the amout of 59 pounds, 2
shillings, and 4 pence. Signed July 2, 1788.

DECEMBER COURT, 1788
Court ordered SAMUEL WEBSTER (of Samuel) and MICHAEL WEBSTER to
answer the complaint of JAMES RENSHAW, and summoned JOHN
BARNEY to testify for the plaintiff. JOHN BARNEY stated
that he heard SAMUEL WEBSTER, SR. say he had sold a parcel
of land to JAMES RENSHAW and he had received part of the
money (he did not recollect how much), and he had sold the
land to another person.
Court ordered the bond given to SAMUEL DURHAM, deceased, in the
name of BUCHANAN & COWAN for the sum of 654 pounds, 7
shillings and 9 pence, dated September 12, 1774, be struck
off the Inventory or List of Debts of the said Durham, and
that Cowan pay the balance due on the books of Buchanan &
Cowan to the executor of said Durham.
Court granted an order be given to JAMES HOLMES for the
maintenance and support of JOHN HOWARD, a maimed and
disabled soldier of Col. Nicola's Corps of Invalids, from
February, 1788 to October 8th next following, 8 months
lacking 4 days. Order for 9 lbs., 16 sh., 2 p.
GREENBERRY DORSEY and JAMES GILES to show cause why ROBERT
BURNEY LENDRUM had not fully administered the goods and
credits of GEORGE READ, late of Harford County, dec'd.
Appeared, but "nothing done in this matter."
MARY HUDSON to show cause why she had not administered on the
goods, chattels and credits of WILLIAM HUDSON, deceased,
and to answer complaint of ALEXANDER COWAN.
RICHARD KREUSON and REBECCA LENDRUM ordered to deliver the
inventory of goods and chattels of GEORGE READ, dec'd.,
with the list of sales of said goods and chattels, and to
answer the complaint of WILLIAM READ.
Court appointed JOSIAS WILLIAM DALLAM and JACOB FORWOOD to
estimate the yearly value of the real estate of GEORGE
COPELAND, deceased, in the company of a Court Justice.
Court ordered the balance of WILLIAM SNELSON's estate to be
charged to the estate of WILLIAM HOLLIS, deceased, and to
pay a dividend from the first estate to MARY PIBUS.

APRIL COURT, 1789
Justices: JOHN LOVE, THOS. BOND, WM. SMITHSON and WM. SMITH.
Court appointed HENRY GREEN as guardian of ELIZABETH GREEN,
MARTHA GREEN, SARAH GREEN and SUSANNAH GREEN, daughters of
LEONARD GREEN, deceased. Securities were BENNETT BUSSEY
and JAMES BARTON. Court ordered distribution of the estate

to the guardian of these children, and MARY GREEN (who is
of age) to get her share in her own hand.
ROBERT BURNEY LENDRUM to show cause why he had not fully
administered the goods, chattels and credits of GEORGE
READ, and to answer the complaint of WILLIAM READ.
MARY HUDSON to show cause why she had not fully administered the
goods, chattels and credits of WILLIAM HUDSON, and to
asnswer the complaint of ALEXANDER COWAN.
ROBERT DUTTON to show why he had not paid FILLISANY WALTHOM that
part of her father's estate left in the hands of JOHN
HUGHSTON of whose last will he is executor, and to also
answer the complaint of ELIZABETH WALTHOM.
ELIZABETH LEE, executrix of JAMES LEE, to answer complaint of
JOSIAS LEE and SAMUEL WEBSTER (of Isaac).
Court ordered WILLIAM HOLLIS, administrator of the goods,
chattels and credits of WILLIAM HOLLIS, deceased, to have
the bonds struck out of the inventory and, further
agreeable to the prayer of the plaintiff, ordered that
HENRY VANSICKLE and JOHN HALL make distribution of the
widow's third out of the estate of WILLIAM HOLLIS.
Court awarded to JAMES SCOTT, a maimed soldier of the First
Maryland Regiment, 7 pounds, 10 sh., up to Feb., 1789.
Court appointed MAJ. JOHN TAYLOR guardian to EDWARD TAYLOR and
ELIZAR TAYLOR, children of EDWARD TAYLOR, deceased.
Approved securities were WILLIAM AMOS and THOMAS POTEET (of
James). Court appointed MAJ. SAMUEL CALWELL and BENJAMIN
B. NORRIS to appraise the goods and chattels.

MAY COURT, 1789
The executors of WILLIAM AMOSS, deceased, were ordered to answer
the Bill in Chancery brought by CHARLES BAKER.
A bond due from ....AMOS to JOHN DALE was ordered to be
settled as to time of payment mentioned in said bond.

JUNE COURT, 1789
ROBERT BURNEY LENDRUM to show cause why he had not fully
administered the goods, chattels and credits of GEORGE
READ, and to answer the complaint of WILLIAM READ.
MARY HUDSON to show cause why she had not administered to the
estate of WILLIAM HUDSON, and to answer complaint of
ALEXANDER COWAN. "Did not appear--said sick."
ELIZABETH LEE to answer the complaint of JOSIAS LEE and SAMUEL
WEBSTER (of Isaac).
Court appointed (with consent of parties) DR. JOHN ARCHER and
CAPT. BENNETT MATHEWS to audit and settle a matter in
dispute between ELIZABETH CREITON, executrix of the last
will and testament of JOHN CREITON, and PATRICK CREITON,
respecting the estate of said JOHN CREITON.
Court allowed EDWARD CAIN, a maimed soldier of the Fourth
Maryland Regiment, his half-pay of eleven pounds and five
shillings, up to June, 1789.
THOMAS WALTHOM HUGHSTON, aged 14 years, came into Court and
chose SAMUEL RICKETTS, JR., as his guardian. Approved
securities were ROGER MATHEWS and MOSES MAXWELL.
MARY HUDSON to show cause why she had not administered on the
estate of WILLIAM HUDSON, and to answer complaint of
ALEXANDER COWAN. Reportedly sick and not able to appear,

but she offered to give up the property to the creditors, according to EDWARD PRIGG, Deputy Sheriff.

BENJAMIN TOLAND to answer complaint of JOHN CHRISTESON. Court ordered BENJAMIN TOLAND to return a list of the debts to the estate of ADAM TOLAND.

ROBERT BURNEY LENDRUM to show cause why he had not fully administered the goods, chattels and credits of GEORGE READ, dec'd., and to answer complaint of WILLIAM READ.

SAMUEL GRIFFITH, executor of MARTHA GARRETSON in account with the heirs of GEORGE GARRETSON, reported his account, including money received from WILLIAM HILL, JOHN BROWN, and SAMUEL HOWELL. He also distributed the the amount of 215 pounds, 4 shillings and 11 3/4 pence each heir, as follows: MR. JOSIAS HALL, for his wife's share; DR. ELIJAH DAVIS, for his wife's share; and, ELIZABETH GARRETSON for her share.

ELIZABETH LEE to answer the complaint of JOSIAH LEE and SAMUEL WEBSTER (of Isaac).

Court approved (with consent of parties) JOHN LEE GIBSON and CAPT. BENNETT MATHEWS to settle the dispute between ELIZABETH CREITON, executrix of JOHN CREITON, and PATRICK CREITON, regarding the estate of JOHN CREITON.

THOMAS WALTHOM HUGHSTON, aged 15 years, came into Court and chose SAMUEL RICKETTS, JR. as his guardian. Approved securities were ROGER MATHEWS and MOSES MAXWELL.

AUGUST COURT, 1789

Court issued an attachment for ROBERT BURNEY LENDRUM for contempt against the Court for not showing cause as to why he had not fully administered the goods, chattels and credits of GEORGE READ, deceased, and for not answering the complaint of WILLIAM READ.

JOSIAS and MARTHA CLEMENTS to answer the complaint of JOHN TAYLOR, guardian to orphans of EDWARD TAYLOR, dec'd.

Court allowed the account of Messrs. RUMSEY and COWAN with respect to the last will and testament of JOHN DAY (of Edward), as follows: For support of family (54 pounds, 9 shillings, 7 1/2 pence); For the widow of JOHN DAY (78 pounds, 10 shillings, 9 pence); For the funeral expenses: 18 pounds, 10 shillings, 9 pence. Approved.

Court approved securities JAMES FISHER and ALEX FISHER to handle the administration of the goods, chattels and credits of WILLIAM FISHER, deceased, in the place of JOSEPH MILLER.

THOMAS STEEL offered WILLIAM MONTGOMERY as his security for due administration of the goods, chattels and credits of THOMAS STEEL, deceased, and released the executors of WILLIAM FISHER who had posted bond for said Steel's executors. The Court approved WILLIAM MONTGOMERY.

Court appointed WILLIAM MORGAN, JOSEPH MILLER, ROBERT HARRIS and JOHN BARCLAY, Esq. to audit and settle a dispute between the executors of WILLIAM FISHER, deceased, and the executors of JOHN JOLLEY, deceased.

Contempt order passed again to attach ROBERT BURNEY LENDRUM.

Court summoned CHARLES JOHNSON, ARCHIBALD HEAPS and HUGH DORAN to testify on the sums of money to be paid to WILLIAM SMITH as executor of BENJAMIN RICHARDSON, at the request of BENJAMIN B. NORRIS. All appeared and CHARLES JOHNSON paid 11 pounds, 17 shillings, 1 pence; ARCHIBALD HEAPS paid 12 pounds, 4 shillings, 9 pence; and, HUGH DORAN paid 7 pounds, 11 shillings, 5 pence.

ARCHIBALD BATEY summoned to testify on his knowledge of the
    controversy between WILLIAM READ and FRANCIS O'NEAL.
THOMAS TIMMONS to answer the complaint of EDWARD TIMMONS.
MARY FORD, administratrix of BENJAMIN FORD, to answer the
    complaint of ROBERT SCOTT, administrator de bonis non of
    JOHN DORNEY.
Court appointed SARAH HALL, WILLIAM HALL and AQUILA HALL as
    guardians of the children of JOHN BEEDLE HALL, dec'd., viz:
    HETTE HALL, aged 10 years on December 24, 1789; EDWARD
    HALL, aged 7 years in July, 1789; DELIA HALL, aged 3 years
    on April 14, 1790; and, AQUILA HALL, aged 2 years on July
    13, 1790. Approved securities were EDWARD HALL and ROGER
    BOYCE.
Court awarded half-pay in the amount of 12 pounds, 10 sh. up to
    August 8, 1789, for JOHN HOWARD, a maimed soldier.
Court awarded half-pay in the amount of 15 pounds for one year
    up to September 14, 1789, to VALLENTINE SMITH, a maimed
    soldier of Col. Nicola's Corps of Invalids.
Court appointed ISAAC WEBSTER and JOHN BARCLAY, Esq., to audit
    the unsettled accounts between the executrix of ROBERT
    COOK, deceased, and ALEXANDER EWING.
Court allowed 20 pounds to administrators of THOMAS RENSHAW.

NOVEMBER COURT, 1789
ELLEANOR........(late McCURDY) to show cause why she had not
    finally settled the estate of ARCHIBALD McCURDY, and to
    answer the complaint of COL. JOHN ROGERS.
THOMAS ELLIOTT to show cause why he had not finally settled the
    estate of THOMAS ELLIOTT, deceased, and to answer the
    complaint of ANN ELLIOTT.
MARY BROWN, widow of JOSHUA BROWN, to answer the complaint of
    FREEBORN BROWN.
BARNARD PRESTON, SR. to answer the complaint of HENRY RUFF and
    HENRY WATTERS, JR., administrators of the goods and
    chattels of JOHN BULL. "The Court is of the opinion that a
    still in partnership between BARNARD PRESTON SR. and JOHN
    BULL, deceased, that the said Bull's part or share of said
    still is and ought to be the property of his
    representatives."
MARY FORD to answer the complaint of ROBERT SCOTT.
WILLIAM BULL, orphan of JOHN BULL, came into Court and chose
    HENRY RUFF, tanner, as his guardian. HENRY WATTERS, SR. and
    RICHARD RUFF were approved as securities.
Court permitted SAMUEL LEE to take an infant child (a child of
    DR. JAMES LEE, son of the said SAMUEL LEE) and the estate
    of the said child by the said Lee's own offer to care at no
    expense for its support or maintenance.

JANUARY COURT, 1790
Justices present: JOHN LOVE, THOMAS BOND, WILLIAM SMITH and
    WILLIAM SMITHSON.
Court approved the account of WILLIAM COULTROUGH as guardian for
    SAMUEL BAYLIS, orphan of BENJAMIN BAYLIS, for the rent of
    his plantation, 259 pounds.
EDWARD KAIN (CAIN), a soldier, to make known to the Court where
    he was wounded, at what place, and who commanded.
JOHN LOWREY, a soldier, to make known to the Court where he was
    wounded, at what place, and who commanded. Appeared in
    Court and said that he served in 1st Maryland Regt. under

Colonel Smallwood and he was wounded through the groin in the Battle of Long Island on August 27, 1776.

VALLENTINE SMITH, a soldier, to make known to the Court where he was wounded and what part.

JOHN JOHNSON to answer the complaint of FRISBY DORSEY and THOMAS GREENFIELD. Matter postponed until March 1st.

MARCH COURT, 1790

Court appointed JAMES BOND and THOMAS GIBSON to audit and settle the estate of BENJAMIN RICHARDSON, deceased, and look into a dispute between WINSTON SMITH, executor of the deceased, and BENJAMIN B. NORRIS, and report same.

PROVIDENCE KITELY, aged 15 years on August 5, 1790, came into Court and chose CHARLES WATERS as her guardian. Securities were WILLIAM SMITH, Esq. and JAMES LYTLE.

ELIZABETH KITELY, aged 13 years (no birth date given) and MARY KITELY, aged 9 years on March 13, 1790 were placed under the guardianship of CHARLES WATERS by the Court.

Court awarded the sum of 12 pounds, 6 shillings for the nine months from February 1 to November 1, 1790, to JAMES SCOTT, a maimed soldier of the 1st Maryland Regiment.

JOHN RUMSEY's Report to the Court, dated February 10, 1783, (essentially as follows): On January 10, 1783, JOHN RUMSEY (Justice of the Peace) and WILLIAM CULTROUGH (guardian for SAMUEL BAYLIS, the eldest son and heir at law of BENJAMIN BAYLIS, dec'd.), with CHARLES GILBERT and FREEBORN BROWN (two persons of good repute and well skilled in building and plantation affairs, neither of them being of kin, indebted or otherwise interested in either the orphan or guardian), entered upon the lands and plantation of SAMUEL BAYLIS and viewed the dwelling houses, out houses, land, orchards and fences on said plantation. After they (CHARLES GILBERT and FREEBORN BROWN) took their oaths upon the Holy Evangelists as administered by said JOHN RUMSEY made a just estimation of the annual value of the plantation of SAMUEL BAYLIS and (in the process of so doing leaving the guardian with a sense of his own responsibility for the quality and quantity of uncleared land for the benefit of the heir when at age to possess said lands and plantation). CHARLES GILBERT and FREEBORN BROWN entered upon the lands of SAMUEL BAYLIS, eldest son and heir at law of BENJAMIN BAYLIS, deceased, and found the following: one dwelling house in good repair; kitchen in good repair; smoke house in good repair; barn, shop and spring house in bad order and repair; weaving shop in good order and repair; two orchards of apple trees (225 young bearing trees and about 20 old trees); about 160 peach trees; fences in medling order and repair; all worth a yearly rent of 37 pounds in their estimation. The guardian is allowed to clear 7 acres of woodland and raise the rent accordingly. Signed CHARLES GILBERT and FREEBORN BROWN, Jan. 10, 1783, and JOHN RUMSEY attested, Feb. 10, 1783.

JOHN RUMSEY's Report to the Court, dated July 23, 1782, (essentially as follows): JOHN RUMSEY (Justice of the Peace) and BENJAMIN RUMSEY (appointed guardian of MOSES MAXWELL, son of CAPT. JAMES MAXWELL, deceased), along with GEORGE PRESBURY and JOHN DORSEY (two persons of good repute and well skilled in building and plantation affairs)

entered the lands of MOSES MAXWELL as devised by the last
will of testament of his deceased father, CAPT. JAMES
MAXWELL, and after administering the oath, said GEORGE
PRESBURY and JOHN DORSEY viewed the lands and buildings so
as to determine their yearly value, viz: two old log
dwelling houses; log kitchen; corn house; about 50 apple
trees; houses and fences in bad repair; all worth a yearly
rent of 25 pounds. Signed by GEORGE PRESBURY and JOHN
DORSEY. Attested: JOHN RUMSEY.
JOHN RUMSEY's Report to the Court, dated July 23, 1782, was
essentially the same as the above report in behalf of MOSES
MAXWELL. This report, in behalf of JACOB MAXWELL, son of
CAPT. JAMES MAXWELL, was handled by the same men as
follows: one tolerable log dwelling house; three old log
dwelling houses in bad repair; corn house and some others
in ruins; fences in bad repair; nearly 50 apple trees
declining there; all worth a yearly rent of 20 pounds.
Signed and attested by the aforementioned men.
JOHN RUMSEY's Report to the Court, dated July 23, 1782, was
essentially the same as the above reports, except that this
valuation was for land devised to JAMES MAXWELL, the late
brother of MOSES MAXWELL and JACOB MAXWELL, all of whom
were sons of CAPT. JAMES MAXWELL, deceased. They reported
the following: one brick dwelling house unfinished; one
small old log dwelling house; one kitchen; one old corn
house; one meat house; four orchards of about 290 apple
trees; the houses except two or three or in midling repair;
all worth a yearly rent of 38 pounds. Valuation signed by
GEORGE PRESBURY and JOHN DORSEY, and attested by JOHN
RUMSEY.
JOHN LOVE's Report to the Court, dated February 12, 1787, was
essentially as follows: JOHN LOVE (Justice of the Peace)
along with HENRY GREEN and BENJAMIN GREEN, who were
appointed by the Court to valuate the real estate of HENRY
THOMAS, JR., deceased, entered said lands and after taking
their oath, viewed the land and buildings as follows: land
was chiefly cleared and much worn, and the building and
other improvements much out of repair; no more land ought
to be cleared or timber cut, and the executor or guardian
put the building and improvements in reasonable repair;
annual rent at this time is only worth 7 pounds, 10
shillings. Signed by HENRY GREEN, BENJAMIN GREEN, JOHN LOVE
and J. GEO. BRADFORD, Regtr.
DANIEL TREDWAY, WILLIAM BRADFORD, SIAS BILLINGSLEY and JOHN COX
reported to the Court that their opinion was that in the
matter between PETER SMITH and the heirs and executors of
JOHN COOK, said PETER SMITH is due the sum of 2 shillings,
3 pence farthing, as of March 28, 1787.

APRIL COURT, 1790
HUGH KIRKPATRICK to answer complaint of the representatives of
ROBERT YOUNG, late of Harford County, deceased.
EDWARD KAIN (CAIN), a disabled soldier, to inform the Court when
and where he was wounded, and who commanded. He appeared
and stated he was wounded in the arm while serving in the
4th Maryland Regiment under Col. Hall.
VALLENTINE SMITH, a maimed soldier, to inform the Court when and
where wounded, and who commanded. (No appearance.)

WILLIAM and MARY ROBINSON to answer the complaint of WILLIAM
    JOHNSON, administrator de bonis non of JOHN COOK. Court
    ordered the estate of JOHN COOK be sold to pay debts.
MARY BROWN (widow of JOSHUA BROWN) to answer the complaint of
    FREEBORN BROWN. Court ruled in favor of defendant.
ELY JARRETT came into Court and chose ABRAHAM JARRETT as his
    guardian. Security: ARCHIBALD ROBINSON & ZACHEUS ONION.
THOMAS GILES and PHILIP COALE, executors of JACOB GILES, to show
    cause why they have not returned an inventory and fully
    settled the deceased's estate, and to answer the complaint
    of WILLIAM SMITH (Bay Side).
(These entries appear to be made in the ledger out of order)
    July 9, 1790, received of HUGH WHITEFORD, executor of HUGH
    WHITEFORD, sum of 20 pounds. Signed JACOB GIBSON. October
    7, 1790, received from HUGH WHITEFORD, executor of HUGH
    WHITEFORD, sum of 100 pounds, it being in full of all
    demands against him. Signed by ANNA WHITEFORD. Witnessed by
    WILLIAM JOHNSTON.
THOMAS WRIGHT, administrator of the goods and chattels of BLOYCE
    WRIGHT, to answer complaint of his securities.
SUSANNAH HUGHES, aged 14 years on September 20, 1790, came into
    Court and chose ROBERT GLEN as her guardian. Security:
    DANIEL SCOTT, JAMES CLENDENNEN (CLENDENNING).
Court appointed JAMES CLENDENNING as guardian of GEORGE HUGHES,
    aged 12 years on April 25, 1790, and MARTHA HUGHES, aged 10
    years on November 1, 1790. Securities were WILLIAM JONES
    and ROBERT GLEN.
JOSEPH HUGHES, aged 19 years in March, 1790, came into Court and
    chose ROBERT GLEN as his guardian. Securities were
    BENJAMIN PRESTON and JAMES CLENDENNEN (CLENDENNING).

AUGUST COURT, 1790
JAMES TAYLOR, aged 15 years (no birth date given) came into
    Court and chose RICHARD MONK as his guardian. Offered
    JAMES WETHERALL and...........as securities; approved.
THOMAS WRIGHT, administrator of BLOYCE WRIGHT, deceased, to
    answer the complaint of his securities. Appeared.
ROBERT TAYLOR and AMOS CORD to show cause why the estate of
    AMASA TAYLOR had not been fully settled and to answer the
    complaint of MATHEW DORSEY. Both appeared.
Court issued an attachment for THOMAS GILES, one of the
    executors of JACOB GILES, to show cause why he had not
    returned an inventory of the estate, and for contempt.
    Appeared. Court adjourned until next week.
JACOB BULL, son of JOHN BULL, aged 16 years on October 13, 1790
    came into Court and chose HENRY RUFF his guardian. JOHN
    DALLAM and JOHN BULL were approved as securities.
Court appointed DR. JOHN ARCHER, JOHN WILSON (merchant), and
    JOHN COX to settle all accounts subsisting between the
    estate of WILLIAM COX and JOSEPH HUSBANDS, both dec'd.
Court ordered JAMES RIGBIE to administer on his father's estate
    (Securities: SAMUEL WALLACE, THOMAS CHEW and JOSEPH MILLER)
    and if not done in two weeks, letters will be issued to ANN
    RIGBIE; if not done in one week, then letters will be
    granted to some other person who can guarantee good
    security.

OCTOBER COURT, 1790
PHILIP COALE, one of the executors of JACOB GILES, deceased, to
    show cause why the estate had not been settled.

41

GEORGE GOLDSMITH PRESBURY to answer the complaint of GEORGE
    PRESBURY (of William).
SAMUEL GRIFFITH to answer the complaint of GEORGE PRESBURY (of
    William).
VOLLINE SMITH and wife to answer the complaint of JOHN
    MONTGOMERY.
CORBIN COULTER to show cause why the estate of THOMAS COOLEY had
    not been fully settled, and to answer the complaint of
    WILLIAM ENSOR.
WILLIAM ALLENDER, executor of JOHN CLARK JENKENS, to answer the
    complaint of the representatives of the deceased.
JAMES BARNETT, executor of MANASSA FINNEY, to answer the
    complaint of ROBERT SCOTT.
GEORGE AMOS to testify to the truth of his knowledge in a matter
    of controversy between the trustees of the estate of JOSHUA
    AMOS and FREDERICK AMOS.
Valuation of the real estate of GEORGE COPELAND, deceased, by
    GREENBERRY DORSEY, Justice of the Peace, and JOSIAS WILLIAM
    DALLAM and JAMES OSBORN, two persons of good repute, all of
    whom entered the property of said GEORGE COPELAND on
    October 9, 1790 and viewed the following: 250 or 300 acres
    of cleared land appearing to be very poor under fence, 6 or
    8 acres of sorry meadow, a young orchard of 130 apple trees
    6 or 7 years old, remnants of an old orchard, an old paled
    garden much rotten, a brick dwelling house with cracked
    walls and a 17 year old roof otherwise in midling repair, a
    brick kitchen, a frame granery and spring house, meat house
    and negro quarters, a log barn and stable with a corn house
    with both having rotten logs and roofs with holes, a house
    occupied as a store in good repair, an old farm house by
    the creek nearly rotten. They also mention more land to be
    cleared near the post road and dead timber to be made use
    of (but no green timber). Annual rent valued at 51 pounds.
    Signed by JOSIAS WILLIAM DALLAM and JAMES OSBORN. Attest:
    JACOB FORWOOD (not GREENBERRY DORSEY).
Court appointed CAPT. SAMUEL GILPIN to divide the lands of
    WILLIAM HUSBANDS, deceased, among his representatives.
BENJAMIN CAMPBELL, aged 14 years on July 20, 1790, chose WILLIAM
    SLADE (of Ezekiel)) his guardian, with EZEKIEL SLADE and
    LEMUEL HOWARD approved as securities.
Court allowed WILLIAM SMITH and ANN RIGBIE, administrators of
    the goods, chattels and credits of JAMES RIBGIE, to sell
    said goods and to give nine months credits.
Court ordered the estate of BENJAMIN CAMPBELL be delivered up
    into the hands of WILLIAM SLADE, his guardian.
Court summoned JOHN LOWREY, WILLIAM HOW, JAMES CLARK, and JANE
    LEWIS to testify for ROBERT SCOTT (plaintiff) against JAMES
    BARNETT (defendant), and JOSEPH BARNETT and JAMES BARNETT,
    SR. to testify for the defendant.
JAMES BARNETT, executor of MANASSA FINNEY, to have his account
    docked and two amounts struck out amounting to fourteen
    pounds, eleven shillings and six pence.
Court summoned EDWARD PRALL, IGNATIUS WHEELER and ISAAC MASSEY
    to testify for WILLIAM SMITH, administrator of the goods
    and chattels of JAMES RIGBIE.
Court accepted THOMAS McGAUGH to be the security for the
    administration of the estate of JAMES CAMPBELL, and
    released JOHN MONTGOMERY.

Court ordered the specific articles in a bill of sale or deed of
    gift from JAMES RIGBIE to SAMUEL WALLACE be struck out of
    the inventory of his goods and chattels.

DECEMBER COURT, 1790
Justices THOMAS BOND and WILLIAM SMITHSON present. Court was
    adjourned until January 17, 1791.

JANUARY COURT, 1791
HANNAH CAMPBELL to answer the complaint of WILLIAM SLADE.
THOMAS WEST to answer the complaint of DAVID THOMAS.
GEORGE LEWES to answer the complaint of DAVID THOMAS.
ENOS WEST to answer the complaint of DAVID THOMAS.
FRANCES WEST to answer the complaint of DAVID THOMAS.
JOHN HANSON to answer the complaint of MARTHA GALLION.
THOMAS BIRCKHEAD to show cause why he had not administered the
    goods, chattels and credits of SAMUEL BIRCKHEAD according
    to the terms of his will, and to answer the complaint of
    ROBERT AMOS. Letters taken by THOMAS HOWEL BIRCKHEAD
    according to the terms and effects of his father's will.

FEBRUARY COURT, 1791
Court Justices divided the real estate of WILLIAM HUSBANDS,
    deceased, among his representatives: RACHAEL HUSBANDS to
    have one half of the plantation where the deceased WILLIAM
    HUSBANDS lived (173 1/2 acres, and in the metes and bounds
    it mentioned MARGARET DALLAM's smith's shop, and tract
    bought of RICHARD DALLAM). MARY HUSBANDS to have the
    plantation on Deer Creek which the deceased had bought from
    JAMES RIGBIE, and also the warehouse at Smith's Ferry on
    the Susquehanna River. WILLIAM BAGLEY for his wife's
    dividend, 160 acres of the land where WILLIAM HUSBANDS
    lived. ELIZABETH HUSBANDS to have a tract laying on Broad
    Creek that was bought by her father from ZACHARIAH BROWN.
    Signed by SAMUEL GILPIN and witnessed by EDWARD JOLLEY on
    November 30, 1790, and reported in Court on February 22,
    1791. (Ed. Note: WILLIAM BAGLEY had married SUSANNAH
    HUSBANDS in 1790.)
GEORGE GOULDSMITH PRESBURY to answer the complaint of GEORGE
    PRESBURY (of William). The record said the contending
    parties undertook to settle things among themselves.
JOHN RUMSEY and GABRIEL CHRISTIE appeared and qualified (as
    Justices) but "not to be in force until March 1, 1791."
JOHN RUMSEY and WILLIAM SMITH were present on March 8, 1791, but
    Court was adjourned until April 12, 1791.

APRIL COURT, 1791
HANNAH CAMPBELL to answer the complaint of WILLIAM SLADE.
SUCKEY RIGBIE (a Negro) to show cause why the Letters of
    Administration on the goods and chattels of POMPEY
    WORTHINGTON (a Negro) should not be revoked. Result: The
    Letters were revoked by a decree of the Court.
FRANCIS WEST, THOMAS WEST, ENOS WEST and GEORGE LEWES to answer
    the complaint of DAVID THOMAS.
JOHN DAUGHETY (DAUGHERTY) came into Court and chose BENJAMIN
    BRUSEBANKS as his guardian, and NORRIS LESTER and WILLIAM
    LESTER were approved as his securities.

Court appointed GREENBERRY DORSEY, HENRY VANSICKLE and JOHN HALL
to lay off the thirds of the lands of GEORGE DAUGHERTY,
deceased, for the use of his widow, MARGARET WHEELER.

MAY COURT, 1791
ISAAC PERRYMAN to answer the complaint of THOMAS HARGROVE.
RICHARD HARGROVE and HELLEN FISHER to testify for the
defendant. The Court judged the nuncupative will of JOHN
FITZGARRALD to be null and void.
JOHN TAYLOR, Esq., to answer the complaint of ISAAC WEBSTER and
DANIEL SHERIDINE, executors of the last will and testament
of NATHAN RIGBIE, deceased.
ARTHUR MONAHAN and JOSEPH HAYS were summoned to testify to the
truth of their knowledge in a matter of controversy between
JOHN McADOW and HUGH KIRKPATRICK.
Court to hear the case involving the administratrix of the goods
and chattels of GEORGE DAUGHERTY, dec'd., and the
indemnifying of JOHN RUFF and JAMES OSBORN (next term).

JUNE COURT, 1791
WILLIAM GROVES to answer the complaint of SAMUEL LYNCH. (Record
was noted that the case was "countermanded.")
MARY FORD to show cause why she had not returned an inventory of
goods and chattels of BENJAMIN FORD according to her
Letters of Administration. (She appeared and returned same,
dated June 13, 1791.)

AUGUST COURT, 1791
Justices: JOHN RUMSEY, WILLIAM SMITH, and GABRIEL CHRISTIE.
ELIZABETH BUSSEY to answer the complaint of WILLIAM HOLLIS,
administrator of WILLIAM HOLLIS, deceased.
JOHN DALLAM, JOSEPH WILSON, JAMES TASKER and ISAAC MASSEY
summoned to testify to the truth of their knowledge of the
last will and testament of JAMES RIGBIE, deceased.
JAMES SCIVINGTON to show cause why he had not delivered up the
goods and chattels of JEREMIAH SULLIVIN now in his
possession, to FRANCES DAUGHERTY, administratrix.
ROBERT WILSON to show cause why he had not delivered up the
goods & chattels of JEREMIAH SULLIVIN in his possession to
FRANCES DAUGHERTY, administratrix of the deceased.
JOHN DURHAM, in behalf of ELIZABETH DURHAM, offered the
nuncupative will of PATRICK McCLOSKY for probate, but DR.
JACOB HALL objected. Also mentioned were ROBERT MONEY,
CYNTHIA THOMPSON, CELIA DURHAM and CHARLES TAIT. The Court
did not allow the probate so A. HALL, counsel for the
defendants, appealed it to the General Court.
MICHAEL NELSON and ABRAHAM GREEN to show cause why they had not
delivered up the goods and chattels of JEREMIAH SULLIVIN to
FRANCES DAUGHERTY, administratrix.
WILLIAM VIRCHWORTH and SARAH VIRCHWORTH to answer complaint of
SAMUEL HOWELL.
DAVID STANDIFORD to testify the truth of his knowledge in a
matter between DANIEL McCOMAS and the executors of JAMES
McCOMAS, deceased.
WILLIAM MONKS, CHARLES TAIT, GEORGE EASTON, JAMES PRICE, EVAN
THOMAS and wife, and JOHN TRULOCK summoned to testify the
truth of their knowledge in a matter between DR. JACOB HALL
and JOHN DURHAM. Sworn for the defendant were CYNTHIA

THOMPSON, CELIA DURHAM, MARY THOMPSON, ROBERT MONEY, JOSIAS
SMITH and FRANCIS CARTY. The Court ruled that the
nuncupative will of PATRICK McCLOSKEY would not be allowed
as legal.
Court ordered the Administrator De Bonis Non of the goods and
chattels of JOHN BEEDLE HALL to sell as much of the
personal property sufficient to pay deceased's debts.
MARGARET DORAN and PHILIP DORAN came into Court and chose JOHN
DORAN their guardian. PATRICK DORAN and JAMES CLENDENNEN
were approved as securities.
Statement of ELIZABETH HUSBAND entered into Court records,
stated the real estate of her father WILLIAM HUSBAND,
deceased, was divided among his heirs on November 30, 1790
by CAPT. SAMUEL GILPIN who was appointed to do so by the
Court, but since she had been hindered by her father's will
to not receive her share until age 18, "which age I am now
past," she wanted the matter put on the record "for fear
any disputes in future may arise about my age." Signed by
ELIZABETH HUSBAND on March 31, 1791, in the presence of
EDWARD PRALL and JOHN BARCLAY.

SEPTEMBER COURT, 1791
JOHN COX, executor of WILLIAM COX, deceased, to show cause why
he had not fully settled the estate of the deceased and to
answer the complaint of ISRAEL COX.
WILLIAM COX, executor of WILLIAM COX, deceased, to show cause
why he had not fully settled the estate of the deceased and
to answer the complaint of ISRAEL COX.
GEORGE CHALK NORRIS to show cause why there were no Letters De
Bonis Non taken out of the estate of EDWARD NORRIS,
deceased, as the former administratrix is also deceased and
the estate had not been fully settled.

DECEMBER COURT, 1791
SAMUEL GOVER and ROBERT GOVER, executors of PRISCILLA GOVER,
deceased, to show cause why they had not returned an
inventory of the deceased's goods and chattels and why they
had not fully settled her estate.
ELIZABETH STEWART to answer complaint of MITCHEL STEWART.
BENJAMIN TOLAND, administrator of ADAM TOLAND, to show cause why
he had not settled the estate of the deceased.
JOSEPH ROBINSON, administrator of GEORGE ROBINSON, to show cause
why the estate of the deceased was not settled.

JANUARY COURT, 1792
Court Justices present: JOHN RUMSEY and WILLIAM SMITH.
ELIZABETH STEWART to answer complaint of MITCHEL STEWART.
MARY FIE, widow of BALTIS FYE, to answer the complaint of
WILLIAM FOWLER. (Name spelled both ways in the record.)
WILLIAM SMITH to answer complaint of EDWARD BARKER and JAMES
STEWARD. Court stated the estate of BENJAMIN AMOS must
stand as it had been heretofore settled by the Court.
RICHARD BIDDLE, orphan of BENJAMIN BIDDLE, came into Court and
chose JOHN BARTON BIDDLE his guardian. ROBERT CLARK and
JOHN SCARF were approved as securities.
Court appointed ROBERT AMOS, SR. and THOMAS HOPE to audit and
settle all matters between RICHARD BIDDLE and JOHN BARTON
BIDDLE as to his guardianship of said Biddle.

MAY COURT, 1792
ELIZABETH STEWART to answer complaint of MITCHEL STEWART. They
    appeared in Court, and the case was dismissed.
MARY FYE to answer complaint of WILLIAM FOWLER.

JUNE COURT, 1792
Justices: JOHN RUMSEY, WILLIAM SMITH and GABRIEL CHRISTIE.
ELIZABETH STEWART to answer complaint of MITCHEL STEWART. They
    appeared and the case was discharged by the Court.
MARY FYE to answer complaint of WILLIAM FOWLER. They appeared in
    Court, but no action was taken.
ROBERT CLARK to answer the complaint of WILLIAM HITCHCOCK
    BARTON. They appeared in Court, but no action taken.
THOMAS POTEET and JAMES POTEET to show cause why they had not
    administered on the goods, chattels and credits of BENJAMIN
    McGUIRE, dec'd., or pay the deceased's debts, and also to
    answer the complaint of FRANCIS O'NEIL.
Court appointed MARTHA WHEELER as the guardian of SUSANNAH
    WHEELER, orphan of JOSIAS WHEELER. EDWARD PRIGG and HENRY
    JOHNS were approved as securities.

AUGUST COURT, 1792
ISRAEL COX against JOHN COX and WILLIAM COX. Court summoned
    JAMES WHITE, FREEBORN BROWN and EUCLIDUS SCARBOROUGH to
    testify for the plaintiff, but no one appeared.
WILLIAM HOOFMAN to answer complaint of ELIZABETH HOOFMAN.
WILLIAM SLADE to answer the complaint of ROBERT BREEDEN.
GARRETT GARRETTSON (of Edward) to answer the complaint of ELIJAH
    BLACKSTON.
JAMES CARROLL against BENJAMIN CARROLL. Court summoned ROBERT
    SAUNDER and SAMUEL COLLINS to testify.
Court certified that ISAAC WEBSTER produced sundry accounts as
    attorney for JOHN BEALE HOWARD, against the estate of JAMES
    MAXWELL, which for want of sufficient vouchers did not pass
    the Court, but the Court also certified that such accounts
    that had proper vouchers did pass.
NATHANIEL HITCHCOCK, aged 17 years in October, 1792, came into
    Court and chose ROBERT CLARK his guardian. Court approved
    ABRAHAM JARRETT and VESEY PRICE as securities.
BENEDICT HITCHCOCK, aged 15 years in February, 1793, came into
    Court and chose ROBERT CLARK his guardian, with ABRAHAM
    JARRETT and VESEY PRICE approved securities.

(Note: There appears to be a duplication of entries for May and
    August, 1792, but the only difference is that one FRANCIS
    O'NEIL is also written down as FRANCIS NEALE.)

JOHN HALL and JAMES GARRETSON were appointed by the Court to
    view and value the estate of the late GEORGE DAUGHERTY, and
    did so as follows: one log dwelling house, 24 X 18, with 2
    cat and clay chimneys, with old floors somewhat decayed,
    with a shingle roof tolerably good, with one kitchen of
    logs nearly decayed; one meat house 12 feet square, with a
    shingle roof about half worn; one old stable with clapboard
    roof nearly decayed; one black- smith shop 16 feet square
    with clapboard roof, gum logs built about 2 years; farm
    contains about 70 acres of cleared land, about 35 acres of
    woodland, the whole under bad fence and in bad condition,

with 55 apple trees; the land is low and swampy and had
been formerly drained but at this time the ditches are
filled up and grown over with bushes and briars, and land
adjoining the fences in the same condition; land has been
cleared in proportion to the tract so no further timber can
be sold off it; annual value appraised at 15 lbs. Report
signed by JOHN HALL and JAMES GARRETSON on May 10, 1791 and
attested by JACOB FORWOOD in Court, Aug. 24, 1792.
WILLIAM HOOFMAN to answer complaint of ELIZABETH HOOFMAN.
     Discharged by the Court by allowing the goods and chattels
     of JOHN ARMSTRONG to be appraised.
SARAH COOK, executrix of ROBERT COOK, to answer complaint of the
     representatives of ALICE SIMS.

SEPTEMBER COURT, 1792
Court appointed JOHN COX and EDWARD PRIGG to audit and settle
     all accounts and disputes subsisting of SAMUEL HENRY and
     JOSEPH HUSBANDS, both deceased.
JOHN BEALE HOWARD, executor of JAMES MAXWELL, to answer the
     complaint of MOSES MAXWELL.
WILLIAM ALLENDER (Baltimore County), administrator of ANN
     ALLENDER, deceased, to show cause why he had not finally
     settled the estate of the deceased.
ANN and THOMAS ELLIOTT to answer complaint of JOHN FORWOOD.
RACHEL COALE to testify the truth of her knowledge in a
     controversy between JOHN COX and WILLIAM COX, executors of
     WILLIAM COX, deceased, and ISRAEL COX.
SAMUEL BOXON ordered to be present at the settling of the matter
     between JOHN B. HOWARD, executor of JAMES MAXWELL, and the
     representatives of said Maxwell.
ROBERT SAUNDERS and SAMUEL STEWART ordered to testify the truth
     of their knowledge in a matter between JAMES CARROLL and
     BENJAMIN CARROLL and their father's will.

FEBRUARY COURT, 1793
RACHEL COALE to testify in the matter between JOHN COX and
     WILLIAM COX, executors of WILLIAM COX, and ISRAEL COX.
WILLIAM GROVES to show cause why he had not fully settled the
     estate of BENJAMIN MEAD according to his will, and to
     answer the complaint of JOS. PERMINTY.
WILLIAM JONES to answer the complaint of ANN MOORE.
WILLIAM WHITEFORD and ROBERT HAWKINS to answer the complaint of
     BENJAMIN JONES.
ROBERT SAUNDERS and SAMUEL STEWART to testify the truth of their
     knowledge in a matter between JAMES CARROLL and BENJAMIN
     CARROLL respecting their father's will.

APRIL COURT, 1793
Justices: JOHN RUMSEY, WILLIAM SMITH and WILLIAM SMITHSON.
GEORGE YORK (Carolina) and wife to answer the complaint of
     NICHOLAS HORNER. (Matter settled between the parties.)
WILLIAM GROVES to show why the estate of BENJAMIN MEAD had not
     been settled and answer complaint of JOS. PERMINTY.
ROBERT SAUNDERS and SAMUEL STEWART to testify to the truth of
     their knowledge in a matter between JAMES CARROLL and
     BENJAMIN CARROLL. Depositions taken of JAMES PRICE, GEORGE
     CUNNINGHAM, and HENRY DAVIS NORRIS.

Court appointed JANE HORNER as guardian of her granddaughter
MARY WATERS, aged 6 years on August 19, 1792. Approved
securities were JACOB BOND and NICHOLAS HORNER.
Court appointed GEORGE YORK as guardian of SARAH SCOTT, aged 2
years in April, 1793, and approved WILLIAM YORK and
NICHOLAS HORNER as securities.

MAY COURT, 1793
GREENBERRY DORSEY and HENRY VANSICKLE took an inventory of the
estate of JOHN BEADLE HALL, Esq., deceased, which was
verified by JACOB FORWOOD, in part: one farm of 360 acres
of old cleared land with mostly old fencing, in the tenure
of JACOB FORWOOD; 4 acres of meadow; an old framed dwelling
house much decayed and scarcely fit to live in; other
buildings are so much decayed that they are not worthy of
mention and best to build new ones; an apple orchard of 130
old trees and a few peach trees and a spoiled garden and
yard nearly gone to decay; all estimated to have a yearly
value of 70 pounds. Another farm in this estate and in the
tenure of CAPTAIN ROGER BOYCE consisted of 157 acres of
cleared land with good common rail fencing; about 4 acres
of meadow; a framed house in tolerable repair except for
the leaking roof; a log kitchen; negro quarters; small
stable in midling repair; other buildings in such repair to
not be worth mentioning; an orchard containing 170 trees;
estimated yearly value of 60 pounds. Also, a mill and old
framed mill house; one pair of colony stones and one pair
of country stones; running gears and wheels appear to be
nearly half worn; boulting chest nearly worn; dwelling
house for the miller nearly decayed; dam of the mill in bad
condition but the race tolerable good; estimated yearly
value of 20 pounds. The appraisers stated that it would not
be in the best interest of the orphans to clear any more
land of green timber, but to use the old timber in making
repairs on these farms, and great care must be taken to
commit no waste. So, they recommended that a small strip of
swamp land be cleared on the farm in possession of JACOB
FORWOOD on the Church Road and extending until it
intersects the corner of the land of AQUILA HALL, Esq.
Reported and signed January 12, 1793.
At the request of JOHN DORAN, the Court appointed JOHN COX and
THOMAS POTEET to appraise the real estate of JOHN DORAN,
PHILIP DORAN and MARGARET DORAN, the last two being minors
and the former being guardian for them, in part: 200 trees
in bad want of pruning and clearing; an old dwelling house
and kitchen gone to decay, not worth repairing; fences in
midling order wanting some repair; some old trees dead and
standing should be cut down and sawn into plank. Annual
valuation of 10 pounds. Report signed on May 16, 1793 and
attested by NATHAN SMITH.
WILLIAM GROVES to answer complaint of JOS. PERMINTY and to show
why estate of BENJAMIN MEAD had not been settled.
EDWARD FLANNAGAN to answer complaint of ANN McLINTICK, and JOHN
CREITON to testify for the plaintiff. (No Return)
JAMES DORNEY to testify the truth of his knowledge in a matter
between NICHOLAS HORNER and the estate of JOSHUA BROWN. (No
Return)
OBRA JONES to answer complaint of WILLIAM NORRIS. Summoned were
JOHN DORNEY, WILLIAM DORNEY and HENRY DORNEY of Baltimore
County. Also, ANN CARROLL, JOSEPH NORRIS, ELIZABETH
SAUNDERS and CATHARINE YATES were summoned.

JAMES TAYLOR came into Court and chose his brother WILLIAM
    TAYLOR as his guardian with RICHARD COALEGATE and JAMES
    DULEY approved as securities.
Court appointed WILLIAM TAYLOR as guardian of SAMUEL TAYLOR,
    with RICHARD COALEGATE and JAMES DULEY as securities.
Court appointed JOHN BARCLAY, Esq., with two freeholders, to
    enter the land of SUSANNAH WHEELER, orphan of JOSIAS
    WHEELER, to estimate the yearly value of the property.

AUGUST COURT, 1793
WILLIAM JOHNSON to answer the complaint of FRANCIS GORDON.
ANN SWART and HANNAH COVENHOVER to testify the truth of their
    knowledge in a matter between JAMES CARROLL and BENJAMIN
    CARROLL respecting their father's will. Case was dismissed.
    The will of JAMES CARROLL established as being valid by the
    Court. Each to pay their own costs.
ROBERT BROWN to answer the complaint of HUGH BAY.
MARY HANSON to answer complaint of GEORGE GALLION & sisters.
OBRA JONES to answer the complaint of WILLIAM NORRIS.

OCTOBER COURT, 1793
Court Justices present: JOHN RUMSEY and WILLIAM SMITH.
Summoned and appeared (nothing further recorded in the Court
    record): GEORGE CUNNINGHAM, SAMUEL STEWART, CATHARINE
    YATES, ELIZABETH SAUNDERS, ANN CARROLL, JOSEPH NORRIS,
    HENRY NORRIS, and MORDECAI DAWS.

NOVEMBER COURT, 1793
PETER BOYER GRACE to answer complaint of REBECCA ASHLEY.
    Appeared in Court; case dismissed.
EDWARD FLANNAGAN to answer complaint of MATTHEW McLINTICK and
    wife. JOHN CREITON to testify for the plaintiff.

DECEMBER COURT, 1793
MOSES JOHNSON to show cause why he had not fully settled the
    estate of RICHARD COOP, of which he is administrator.
CEBELLA COOPER to show cause why she had not fully settled the
    estate of CALVIN COOPER, as she is administratrix.
ROBERT HARRIS and PEIRCE CREIGH to answer the complaint of JAMES
    MONTGOMERY.
SAMUEL BALIS to answer the complaint of NATHIEL BALIS.
Court appointed THOMAS HALL as guardian of JOHN HALL, WILLIAM
    HALL, and NATHAN HALL, orphans of WILLIAM HALL, deceased,
    with AQUILA HALL and WILLIAM HALL securities.

APRIL COURT, 1794
Court Justices present: JOHN RUMSEY and WILLIAM SMITH. THOMAS
    BOND appeared and qualified as a Court Justice.
WILLIAM SMITH (of Robert) and JOHN SMITH (of Robert) to answer
    the complaint of ELIZABETH LINSEY.
JAMES DEAVER to answer the complaint of SARAH DEAVER. Summoned
    to testify were ALEXANDER RIGDON, ISAAC JONES (of William),
    THOMAS.......(no last name given), HENRY RICHARDSON, and
    ISAAC JONES (of Theophilus).
RUTH BUSSEY to answer the complaint of THOMAS JOHNSON.
HENRY GREEN, trustee for HUGH KIRKPATRICK, to answer the
    complaint of JOHN McADOW.

49

Court approved NICHOLAS HORNER and JOSIAS SMITH securities for
WILLIAM DEBRULAR & wife, guardians to MARY KITELEY.
JAMES ARMOND, aged 14 years on May 8, 1793, bound until age 21
to ISAAC WILSON to learn the tanner's and currier's trade,
and read, write and cipher to the rule of three.
JOHN DOFFIN, aged 12 years (no birth date given) bound until age
21 to ROBERT SHAW to learn the weaver's trade, and to read,
write and cipher as far as the rule of three.
JOHN BIRKINS, aged 8 years on December 19, 1783, bound until age
21 to ISAAC WILSON to learn the tanner and curriers trade,
and read, write and cipher to the rule of three. (Record
shows year of birth as 1783, but could be 1793)
MARTHA BIRKINS, aged 14 years on January 29, 1784, bound until
age 16 to ISAAC WILSON to learn to read and write and
receive the usual freedoms upon arrival at age 16. (Record
shows year of birth as 1784, but could be 1794)
JOHN HENDERSON, aged 4 years on September 2, 1783, bound until
age 21 to JOHN McFADDEN to learn the occupation of a
farmer, and read, write & cipher to the rule of 3. (Record
shows year of birth as 1783, but could be 1793)
MARY HENDERSON, aged 4 years on September 29, 1793, bound until
age 16 to JOHN McFADDEN to learn to read & write.
JOHN DIXSON, aged 10 years on May 10, 1794, bound until age 21
to JOHN NORTON to learn the shoemaker's trade, and to read,
write and cipher as far as the rule of three.
BENJAMIN HARRIS, aged 16 years on January 1, 1794, bound until
age 21 to MICHAEL MATHERS to learn the hatter's trade and
to receive 6 months night schooling, with half of his
clothing expense shared by ROBERT HARRIS.
Court ordered HUGH KIRKPATRICK to deliver to JOHN McADOW,
administrator de bonis non of JAMES McADOW, the goods and
chattels of the estate of JAMES McADOW, deceased, to the
amount of 66 pounds, 8 shillings and 2 pence, with interest
from November 1, 1776 accruing.
WILLIAM MORGAN and SAMUEL RAIN came into Court and released
FRANCIS NEIL from his bond for ANNA ALLENDER for the
administration of the estate of WILLIAM ALLENDER.
BENJAMIN CULVER MITCHELL, aged 16 years on May 15, 1794, bound
until age 21 to JOHN MITCHELL to learn the trade of
millwright, and read, write and cipher to rule of 3.
JOHN WOOD, aged 18 years on August 19, 1794, bound until age 21
to JOHN RUMSEY to learn to read, write and cipher as far as
the rule of three.

JUNE COURT, 1794
JAMES DORNEY to answer the complaint of NICHOLAS HORNER.
WILLIAM SMITH (of Robert) and JOHN SMITH (of Robert) to answer
the complaint of ELIZABETH LINDSEY.
ISAAC PERRYMAN to answer the complaint of ELLEANER EGLESTON.
JOHN STREET, JOHN CREITON and BENJAMIN JONES to testify the
truth of their knowledge in a matter of controversy between
SARAH DEAVER and JAMES DEAVER.
JAMES WETHERALL to answer the complaint of JOSEPH HUGHES
PRESBURY.
Certificate from the Clerk of the General Court of the State of
Maryland was received, certifying that the Writ that was
brought by GEORGE BOND, executor of SARAH BOND, against

WILLIAM RICHARDSON and others, had been quashed. Defendants
pay cost: 1098 pounds of tobacco.
JAMES LYTLE and JOHN DURHAM were appointed by JOHN RUMSEY to
enter and appraise the lands, house, orchards, fences, etc.
lately belonging to CHARLES WATERS. They appraised the
yearly value as 50 pounds (no description was given of the
property). Report signed on December 28, 1793.

AUGUST COURT, 1794
JAMES DORNEY to testify the truth of his knowledge in a matter
between the executors of JOSHUA BROWN and NICHOLAS HORNER.
ZEPHENIAH TALLBY, ISAAC COPHRON and STEPHEN WHITE to testify the
truth of their knowledge in a matter between JOSHUA
CUNNINGHAM and HENRY RUFF.
FRISBY DORSEY and MATTHEW DORSEY, administrators of LAWRENCE
OSBORN, to show why an inventory had not been returned.
JAMES BARNES, administrator of JAMES COALE, to show cause why he
had not returned an inventory.
ISAAC JONES (of Theophilus) and JOHN COX to testify the truth of
their knowledge in a matter between JAMES DEAVER and SARAH
DEAVER.
JOHN TAYLOR, supposed to be 10 years old, bound until age 21 to
JAMES GORDON to learn the farming business, and read and
write and cipher as far as the rule of three.
ISAAC WOOD, aged 18 years (no birth date given) bound until age
21 to MATTHEW SNOWDAY to learn the joiner's trade, and to
give him 3 months schooling, and 4 pounds a year for the
first 2 years and 5 pounds for the third year.
GEORGE TAYLOR, aged 16 years on March 1, 1794, bound until age
21 to MICHAEL MATHER to learn the hatter's trade, and
JOSEPH FORD, guardian to GEORGE TAYLOR, agreed to pay him
such freedom dues as customary when he is 21.
JESSE BROWNE, aged 3 years on December 1, 1794, bound until age
21 to DAVID MAULSBY to learn the farming business, and to
read, write and cipher as far as the rule of 3.
Court approved JOHN EVATT as guardian of his son JOHN EVATT, one
of the legatees of WILLIAM EVATT (EVIT), deceased; JAMES
BARNETT and JAMES FISHER approved as securities.
CHARLES NORRIS, aged 18 years on September 7, 1794, bound until
age 21 to JOSHUA DAY to learn the carpenters and joiners
trade, and read, write and cipher to rule of 3.
MARK SWIFT, aged 17 years on October 2, 1794, bound until age 21
to AMOS HOLLIS to learn the farming business and to read,
write and cipher as far as the rule of three.
Certiorari from the General Court of the Western Shore of
Maryland in a case pending between WILLIAM RICHARDSON,
BENJAMIN RICHARDSON, SAMUEL RICHARDSON, JAMES NORRIS,
ROBERT HAWKINS and GEORGE BRADFORD.

SEPTEMBER COURT, 1794
Court Justices: JOHN RUMSEY, WILLIAM SMITH and THOMAS BOND.
JAMES LYTLE and JOHN DURHAM were appointed by JOHN RUMSEY to
enter the property of the late WALTER SCOTT, now in the
possession of GEORGE YORK, guardian, which they did and
valued the land, etc. (no description given) at 13 lbs. per
annum, and added that timber should be cleared for fencing
and cut for firewood as needed, where it is most
convenient. Report signed on December 27, 1793.

HANNAH CAMPBELL to answer the complaint of WILLIAM SLADE.
JOHN CREIGHTON, ALEXANDER MANNERS, and BENJAMIN JONES (of
    Theóphilus) to testify the truth of their knowledge in a
    matter between JAMES DEAVER and SARAH DEAVER. They were
    summoned, appeared, and the Court ruled that it would not
    allow the account of JAMES DEAVER rendered against the
    estate of RICHARD DEAVER, deceased.
ZEPHENIAH TALBY, ISAAC COHRON, STEPHEN WHITE and WILLIAM DURHAM
    (plasterer) to testify the truth of their knowledge in a
    matter between JOSHUA CUNNINGHAM and HENRY RUFF. MARY
    WHITE to testify for HENRY RUFF.
NICHOLAS HORNER to answer the complaint of JOHN DORNEY.
JAMES DORNEY to testify the truth of his knowledge in a matter
    between JOHN DORNEY and NICHOLAS HORNER.
Court appointed MARTHA GRIFFITH as special guardian to JOHN
    GRIFFITH, EDWARD GRIFFITH, LUKE GRIFFITH and ALEXANDER
    GRIFFITH "to take care of the persons of the aforesaid
    children." JOSIAH HALL & GEORGE PATTERSON, securities.
HAMPTON SEREA, aged 3 years on January 31, 1795, bound until age
    21 to AARON BORAM to learn the farming business and to
    receive one year's schooling.
Indenture, dated October 8, 1794, concerning WILLIAM WATTERS who
    bound himself (with consent of his father STEPHEN WATTERS)
    to JOHN MOORES to learn the tanner and currier trade for 4
    years and 6 months. Said Watters was bound to obey his
    master, and shall not play cards, dice or any other
    unlawful game, nor play taverns or ale houses nor
    fornicate, nor shall he commit marriage, nor shall he
    absent himself without his master's permission, and in
    return the master shall teach said Watters his trade and
    keep him in meat and drink and washing and lodging and
    common wearing apparel fit for such an apprentice. Signed
    by WILLIAM WATTERS, STEPHEN WATERS, JOHN MOORES and
    witnessed by WILLIAM SMITHSON, October 8, 1794.

OCTOBER COURT, 1794
MARY WHITE, wife of JONATHON WHITE, to testify the truth of her
    knowledge in a matter between HENRY RUFF and JOSHUA
    CUNNINGHAM.
ZEPHENIAH TALBEY, ISAAC COHRON and JOHN DURHAM (plasterer) to
    testify the truth of their knowledge in a matter between
    JOSHUA CUNNINGHAM and HENRY RUFF.
JOHN McCASKEY to answer the complaint of JOHN DURHAM.
THOMAS DURHAM to answer the complaint of JOHN DURHAM.
ASA TAYLOR to answer the complaint of JOHN DEBRULAR.
GEORGE WESLEY, aged 16 years on September 1, 1794, bound until
    age 21 to JOHN MITCHELL to learn the millwright's trade and
    to read, write and cipher to the rule of 3.

DECEMBER COURT, 1794
Court Justices: JOHN RUMSEY, WILLIAM SMITH and THOMAS BOND.
EDWARD FLANNAGAN to answer complaint of MATTHEW McCLINTICK and
    wife. H. DORSEY summoned for the plaintiff.
ALEXANDER LAWSON SMITH, ELIJAH DAVIS, SAMUEL GRIFFITH and
    FRANCIS GARRETSON to answer the complaint of MARTHA
    GRIFFITH. The Court ordered the executors of SAMUEL
    GRIFFITH to pay costs so far for Clerk and Sheriff.

JAMES McLOCHLIN, aged 12 years on February 15, 1795, bound until
    age 21 to ROBERT McGAY to learn the cooper trade and to
    read, write and cipher as far as the rule of 3.
JOHN DOBBINS, aged 14 years on September 4, 1794, bound until
    age 21 to JOSEPH SAUNDERS to learn the farming business and
    to read, write and cipher to rule of 3.
Court recorded payment of 20 pounds rent for WILLIAM BULL's
    place, paid to HENRY RUFF guardian of WILLIAM BULL in
    January, 1794. Also, WILLIAM BULL acknowledged that he
    received of HENRY RUFF by the hands of HENRY WATERS, SR.,
    60 pounds for the rent of his land, July 26, 1794. Said
    transaction witnessed by JOHN FORWOOD.
Court recorded payment of 9 pounds, 8 shillings and 6 pence to
    THOMAS MILES as guardian of JAMES MILES, August 19, 1794.
    Said transaction witnessed by HENRY RICHARDSON.

FEBRUARY COURT, 1795
Court summoned JAMES MONTGOMERY, PEIRCE CREIGH and ROBERT HARRIS
    to appear. (No Return)
CATHARINE ANDERSON to answer the complaint of JOHN CLARK.
JAMES BARNS, administrator of the goods and chattels of JAMES
    COALE, to show cause why he had not returned an inventory,
    did not appear and was found in contempt.

MARCH COURT, 1795
ALEXANDER L. SMITH, ELIJAH DAVIS, and MARTHA GARRETSON "of the
    last will and testament of SAMUEL GRIFFITH, late deceased,
    etc." to answer complaint of MARTHA GRIFFITH.

APRIL COURT, 1795
ISAAC HENRY and HANNAH HENRY to answer the complaint of WILLIAM
    JAMES.
CATHARINE ANDERSON to answer the complaint of JOHN CLARK.
EDWARD KAIN (CAIN) to answer the complaint of JOHN DORAN and
    PATRICK DORAN. Appeared in Court and case dismissed.
AMOS BARNS to answer the complaint of MITCHELL STEWART.
THOMAS KELLEY, RICHARD GREENLAND and JAMES McCLURE to testify
    the truth of their knowledge in a matter between WILLIAM
    SMITH and JAMES GORREL, executors of ALEXANDER KELLEY.
Indenture, dated February 21, 1795, concerning JOHN WILSON, son
    of JAMES WILSON, who bound himself (with consent of his
    father) to RICHARD SWEANY to learn the chairmaker's trade
    for 7 years and said Wilson shall obey his master at all
    times and shall not play cards or dice or play in taverns
    or ale houses, nor frequent fornication, nor commit any
    matrimonial contract, but in all things behave himself as a
    good and faithful apprentice, and in return, said Wilson
    shall recieve 7 or 8 months tuition from his master, plus a
    complete suit of the best cloth, and as many tools as may
    be necessary to make chairs. Signed by JOHN WILSON, JAMES
    WILSON and RICHARD SWEANY, and acknolwedged by ROBERT
    MORGAN.
Indenture, dated February 28, 1795, concerning JOHN DORSEY of
    Baltimore County who bound himself (with consent of his
    father NICHOLAS DORSEY, farmer of Baltimore County) to
    BENJAMIN MORSEL, carpenter of Harford County, to learn his
    trade for 4 years, and said Dorsey shall obey his master
    and keep his secrets and shall not depart or absent himself
    without his master's permission, and in return said Dorsey

shall be trained as a carpenter and receive meat, drink, washing, lodging, apparel and all other necessaries. Signed by BENJAMIN MORSEL and NICHOLAS DORSEY, and witnessed by JOHN RUMSEY.

AQUILA HUGHES, aged 16 years in June, 1795, bound until age 21 to DANIEL PARSONS to learn the taylor's trade, and to read, write and cipher as far as the rule of three.

JOHN NORRIS, aged 10 years in May, 1795, bound until age 21 to JAMES PERINE to learn the farming business, and to read, write and cipher as far as the rule of three.

CLEMENT WALTHOM came into Court and chose SAMUEL RICKETTS, JR. as his guardian. JAMES LYTLE and HENRY WETHERALL were approved as securities.

Court ordered the executors of SAMUEL GRIFFITH to return a legal inventory within 20 days.

In the matter between MARTHA GRIFFITH and the executors of SAMUEL GRIFFITH, the Court on motion granted leave to withdraw their libel without cost.

HARRY (a Negro boy aged 5 years) was bound until age 21 to THOMAS BOND (of John) to learn the farming business, and to read, write and cipher as far as the rule of 3 and to receive the customary freedom dues when age 21.

Court appointed RICHARD RUFF as guardian of ANN BULL, and approved HENRY WATERS, JR. and WILLIAM BULL securities.

Court ordered some dry hides in the tanyard of HENRY RUFF be sold at private sale, and all leather be sold for the benefit of the estate and administrators of HENRY RUFF.

JUNE COURT, 1795

PEIRCE CREIGH and ROBERT HARRIS to answer the complaint of JAMES MONTGOMERY.

THOMAS KELLEY, RICHARD GREENLAND and JAMES McCLURE to testify the truth of their knowledge in a matter between WILLIAM SMITH and wife and JAMES GORREL and wife, executors of the last will of ALEXANDER KELLEY.

WILLIAM DEBRULAR to answer the complaint of NICHOLAS HORNER.

JAMES DULEY and WILLIAM DULEY to answer the complaint of ALEXANDER McCOMAS.

JAMES OSBORN to answer the complaint of SUSANNAH OSBORN.

GREENBERRY DORSEY and ROBERT TAYLOR summoned to Court in a matter between AMOS BARNES, administrator of the goods etc. of JOHN WOOD, and others.

REASON ROLES, aged 11 years on August 5, 1795, bound until age 21 to WILLIAM MITCHELL, JR. (son of William) to learn the shoemaker's trade, and to read, write and cipher as far as the rule of three.

ELIZABETH MULLEN, aged 6 years on June 25, 1795, bound until age 16 to JOSHUA HUSBANDS to learn to read, spin and do other household business.

HENRY HALL WEBSTER, aged 12 years on October 15, 1794, bound until age 21 to RICHARD HARBERT to learn the weaver's trade, and to read, write and cipher to the rule of 3.

JOHN COPELAND came into Court and chose GEORGE PATTERSON as his guardian. THOMAS HALL and JAMES LYTLE, securities.

CLARK HOLLIS, aged 17 years on April 30, 1795, bound until age 21 to MATTHEW SNOWDAY to learn the carpenter and joiners trade, and to receive three month's schooling, plus 4

pounds, 10 shillings for the first three years and 9 pounds
for the fourth and last year.
WILLIAM ROWLES came into Court & chose WILLIAM MITCHELL, SR. as
his guardian. JAMES MITCHELL & WILLIAM MITCHELL, JR. were
approved as securities.
Application of MARTHA GRIFFITH, widow and relict of SAMUEL
GRIFFITH, deceased. A distribution of one-third part of his
personal estate was ordered for her by the Court.

AUGUST COURT, 1795
Court Justices: JOHN RUMSEY, WILLIAM SMITH and JAMES BOND.
ALEXANDER L. SMITH, ELIJAH DAVIS, SAMUEL GRIFFITH, and MARTHA
GARRETSON were cited. Court record states "the defendants
demand the plenary proceedings by libal."
JAMES DEAVER to answer the complaint of JOHN STREET.
WILLIAM HOLLIS, administrator of WILLIAM HOLLIS, deceased, to
show cause why he had not fully administered the estate,
and to answer complaint of GREENBERRY DORSEY.
PEIRCE CREIGH and ROBERT HARRIS to answer the complaint of JAMES
MONTGOMERY.
JAMES DULEY and WILLIAM DULEY to answer the complaint of
ALEXANDER McCOMAS (James Run).
AMOS BARNES to answer the complaint of MITCHEL STEWART.
GREENBERRY DORSEY and ROBERT TAYLOR to testify to their
knowledge in a matter between AMOS BARNES and others.
JAMES HUTSON to answer the complaint of BENJAMIN CARROLL,
administrator of WILLIAM PROCTOR.
RACHEL (a Negro girl) aged about 13 years, bound until age 16 to
SAMUEL HOPKINS to learn household business and to knit and
spin, with the usual freedom dues when age 16.
Indenture, dated January 28, 1795, concerning PERRY NOLAND, son
of JOHN NOLAND of Harford County, planter, bound with the
consent of his mother to WILLIAM FOWLER to be taught the
craft of cordwainer for a term of 3 years, during which
term the said Noland shall obey his master and he shall not
play cards, dice or any other unlawful game, nor shall he
haunt playhouses or taverns, nor commit fornication, nor
contract matrimony, nor absent himself without his master's
permission, and in return the master shall provide him with
sufficient meat and clothing fitting for an apprentice, and
at the end of his term, said Fowler shall give said Noland
a suit of clothes, a kit of tools, and 10 pounds cash.
Signed by PERRY NOLAND (his mark) and WILLIAM FOWLER.
Witnessed by BENEDICT EDWARD HALL, and recorded May 30,
1795.
GREGORY BARNES, JR. and JANE REESE came into Court and said
JANES REESE bound her son ASEL REESE, aged 6 years on May
1, 1795, to said GREGORY BARNES, JR. to learn the farming
business, and to read, write and cipher to the rule of
three, with customary freedoms at ag 21. Signed by JACOB
FORWOOD and EDWARD PRALL on August 25, 1795.

OCTOBER COURT, 1795
SARAH EDEN and BENJAMIN EDEN to show cause why they had not
fully settled the estate of WILLIAM EDEN, and to answer the
complaint of JAMES ORR.
ELIZABETH CREITEN to answer the complaint of JOHN CREITEN.
JAMES DULEY and WILLIAM DULEY to answer the complaint of
ALEXANDER McCOMAS. (No appearance; attachment ordered)

FRISBY DORSEY and MATTHEW......., administrators of LAWRENCE
    OSBORN, to show why they had not returned an inventory.
    (Case was dismissed upon their returning an inventory.)
GREENBERRY DORSEY to answer complaint of GEORGE PATTERSON.
AMOS BARNS to answer the complaint of MITCHEL STEWART.
SUSANNA OSBORN, CYRUS OSBORN and GEORGE HENDERSON to answer the
    complaint of JAMES OSBORN.
JONATHAN HAMILTON, ANNA MORRISON and ROBERT HAMILTON to prove
    the will of JOHN WINEMAN at the request of the executors of
    IGNATIUS WHEELER. (Appeared; will proven)
ARCHER HAYS to testify to his knowledge in a matter between
    GREENBERRY DORSEY & GEORGE COPELAND's representatives.
Court appointed MARY BROWNE, widow of JOSHUA BROWNE, as the
    guardian to her daughter MARY ANN BROWN (BROWNE) and her
    son JOHN BROWN (BROWNE). JAMES WETHERALL and HENRY
    WETHERALL were approved as securities.
SAMUEL ROBINSON, aged 12 years on April 14, 1795, bound until
    age 21 to JOSHUA DAY to learn the carpenter and joiners
    trade, and read, write and cipher to rule of 3.
Court appointed GEN. JOHN CARLILE and CAPT. ROGER BOYCE to value
    to SARAH COPELAND her share of her father GEORGE COPELAND's
    estate, in the hands of GREENBERRY DORSEY.
Court appointed GODFREY WATERS guardian of JOHN RUFF, orphan of
    HENRY RUFF. HENRY WATERS, SR. and WALTER WATERS were
    approved as securities.
Court appointed HANNAH RUFF as guardian of RICHARD RUFF, GEORGE
    BRADFORD RUFF and HENRY RUFF, orphans of HENRY RUFF. JOHN
    WILSON and WILLIAM WILSON (of William) were approved as
    securities.
Court appointed JOHN STREET guardian of AQUILA DEAVER, with JOHN
    DORAN and JAMES MONTGOMERY approved as securities.

FEBRUARY COURT, 1796
SUSANNA OSBORN, CYRUS OSBORN, GEORGE HENDERSON and ARCHER HAYS
    to testify in a matter between GREENBERRY DORSEY and the
    representatives of GEORGE COPELAND.
SAMUEL HOPKINS MASON (or SAMUEL HOPKINS, mason?) to testify as
    to the truth of his knowledge in a matter between
    GREENBERRY DORSEY and the executors of AQUILA PACA, JR.
JAMES SMITH, executor of THOMAS SMITH, to show cause why the
    estate of the deceased had not been fully settled.
BENJAMIN CARROLL to answer the complaint of JAMES YORK.
ALEXANDER L. SMITH, ELIJAH DAVIS, SAMUEL GRIFFITH, and MARTHA
    GARRETSON, executors of SAMUEL GRIFFITH, to show cause why
    the distribution of the personal estate of the deceased was
    not made agreeable to the prayer of the deceased's widow.
    HENRY DORSEY summoned to testify.
JAMES DULEY and WILLIAM DULEY to answer the complaint of
    BENJAMIN McCOMAS.
HANNAH CAMPBELL to answer the complaint of WILLIAM SLADE.
Indenture, dated January 22, 1796, concerning JOSEPH SMITH, son
    of NATHANIEL SMITH, who was bound with the consent of his
    father to JOSEPH PRIGG to learn the cordwainer's trade for
    a term ending on April 22, 1798, and the said Smith shall
    obey his master and not embezzle or waste his goods, nor
    lend them without consent, nor be absent without his
    master's permission, and in return the said Smith shall
    receive from the said Prigg, meat, drink, washing, lodging
    and apparel and all other necessaries. Signed by NATHAN

56

SMITH and JOSEPH PRIGG (his mark) in the presence of ROBERT
MORGAN and EDWARD PRIGG, and also acknowledged by ROBERT
MORGAN and JOHN BARCLAY.
JOHN CHAUNCY and JAMES GARRETSON were appointed by the Court to
appraise the real estate of JOSEPH EVEREST, deceased known
as "Coheirs Loot" as follows: tract of marsh and wood land
of about 480 acres; one log dwelling house, 20 feet by 18
feet, with a shingle roof and two floors and one outside
chimney made partly of brick and partly of cat and clay,
all in good repair and about 5 years old; one old kitchen
nearly rotten; a small meat house, 12 feet by 14 feet, with
a clapboard roof about 3 years old; "one small house on a
sled", 10 feet by 6 feet, nearly new; one barn, 20 feet
square, with a shingle roof and plank floor in good repair,
about 5 years old; one small cornhouse, 25 feet long and 10
wide, the logs in good repair but the roof worn out; 104
apple trees planted last spring, and a small peach tree
nursery; 150 acres of cleared land much incommoded by
swamps and ponds, divided into 4 fields by indifferent
fences, and within the enclosures there is a large piece of
wood land, and its timber was cut down for bark in the life
of Mr. Everest, and the timber used for rails and fireing
for the use of the farm and the rest sold to enable the
guardian to pay the annual rent and make repairs; no green
timber is to be used while there is sufficient old, except
for rebuilding the cornhouse and the kitchen which the
guardian must do in a workmanlike manner, keeping exact
account of the nails used thereon and the carpenter's bill.
Signed by JOHN CHAUNCY and JAMES GARRETSON on November 15,
1795, and certified by JACOB FORWOOD on January 11, 1796.
HUGH WHITEFORD and JOHN WATKINS were appointed by the Court to
value the land belonging to AQUILA DEAVER, son of JAMES
DEAVER, said land was left him by his grandfather RICHARD
DEAVER, containing 102 acres of which 65 acres are cleared
land; one log house one story high, 16 feet square with
plank floors "above and below but loose;" an apple orchard
originally containing 100 trees, some of which are missing;
annual value estimated to be 16 pounds, and no timber to be
cut except for fences and firewood. Signed by HUGH
WHITEFORD, SR. and JOHN WATKINS, November 26, 1795 and
witnessed by N. SMITH.
SARAH DORNEY came into Court and chose WILLIAM MORRIS her
guardian. Securities: ISAAC WEBSTER & DANIEL ROBINSON.
EDWARD HALL (son of JOHN BEADLE HALL) came into Court and chose
AQUILA HALL his guardian. Approved securities were THOMAS
HALL and FRANCIS HOLLAND.
JAMES COWAN, aged 14 years on August 1, 1796, bound until age 21
to THOMAS COWAN to learn the carpenter's trade, and to
read, write and cipher as far as the rule of 3.
Court bound WILLIAM KEARN (age not recorded) to WILLIAM KIRKWOOD
for 7 years to learn the farming business, and to read,
write and cipher as far as rule of 3.
HUDSON WOOD (age not known) bound until age 21 to MICHAEL MATHER
to be a hatter, and to receive wearing apparel.
THOMAS CRAWFORD, aged 15 years on November 19, 1795, bound until
age 21 to MICHAEL MATHER to be a hatter, and to receive
wearing apparel during his apprenticeship.

ISAAC DULANEY, aged 18 years in March, 1796, bound for three years to JOSEPH EVEREST "to give him fourteen schooling and customary freedom dues." (Note: Apparent error by the clerk in not recording the trade to be learned and other things, as quoted in the awkward wording above.)

AQUILA HALL appeared in behalf of EDWARD KEAN.

BETSEY (a Negro child) aged 4 years, bound until age 16 to ARNEL BUSH to learn to read, spin & do other household business, with customary freedom dues upon reaching 16.

MARCH COURT, 1796

MARTHA DAUGHERTY, aged 4 years on May 15, 1796, bound until age 16 to JOHN REARDON to learn to read, knit, spin, and do other household business.

JOSEPH WALTON, aged 15 years in November, 1796, bound until age 21 to JOSEPH BURGES to learn the trade of cabinet making, to give him 6 months schooling, to allow him to visit his relations every year, and to give him a nice suit of clothes exclusive of his common clothing.

APRIL COURT, 1796

ELIZABETH CRETIN to answer the complaint of JOHN CRETIN.

WILLIAM JOHNSON to answer complaint of the representatives of JOHN COOK.

Court was of the opinion that MARTHA GRIFFITH, widow of SAMUEL GRIFFITH, was entitled to one-third of the personal estate of the deceased and ordered that the distribution be made accordingly.

Court appointed JOHN BAKER as guardian of MARY DEBRULAR, orphan of GEORGE DEBRULAR, with JAMES CARROLL and WILLIAM McCOMAS (of Solomon) approved as securities.

Indenture, dated March 3, 1795, concerning MORDECAI MEADS being bound with the consent of his father JAMES MEADS, JR., to WILLIAM DAVIS HAWKINS to learn the blacksmith trade for the term of November 24, 1794 to November 24, 1797, at which time MORDECAI MEADS will be 21 years old if still living. Said apprentice Meads shall obey his master's lawful command and cause his master to suffer no damage during his apprenticeship, nor play cards or dice or any other unlawful game, nor commit matrimony, nor frequent taverns, ale houses or places of gambling, nor absent himself without his master's permission, and in return said Meads shall receive from said Hawkins training in the blacksmith trade, two months schooling in addition to that already received, and sufficient meat, drink, clothing, lodging and other necessaries. Signed by JAMES MEADS, JR. and WILLIAM DAVIS HAWKINS.

Indenture, dated March 11, 1796, concerning ISAAC BURKIN, son of CHARLES BURKIN, deceased, who was bound with the consent of his mother to JOHN FORWOOD to learn the farmers business and nailers trade until said Burkin reaches age 21 (stated he was born September 8, 1781). Said apprentice Burkin shall obey his master and serve his lawful commands faithfully and not hurt his master, nor shall he sell any of his master's property or lend any of it without his master's knowledge, and he shall not haunt taverns nor contract matrimony during this term, nor absent himself day or night without leave, and in return said Burkin shall receive training as stated, plus sufficient meat, drink, washing, lodging and apparel and other necessaries in both

health and sickness, and to learn to write a legible hand
and to cipher as far as the rule of three, and upon
completion he shall get a new suit of clothes and 5 pounds
money. Signed by JOHN FORWOOD and ISAAC BURKIN (his mark)
and witnesses JOSEPH BUTLER, ROBERT MORGAN, & JOHN BARCLAY.
ELEANOR BURKIN, mother of Isaac, also gave her consent.
JOSIAS HALL and JOHN CHAUNCY were appointed by the Court to
value the real estate of BELCHER MICHAEL, deceased, on
January 1, 1796, as follows: a plantation of 300 acres, 235
of which are cleared and improved; one log dwelling house,
22 feet by 14 feet and sheded on one side, with floors and
chimney all in bad repair and very old; one quarter rotten
and useless; one meat house, 12 feet square with a
clapboard roof 5 years old; one spoiled garden, 100 feet
square, in bad repair and scarcely worth mentioning; one
framed barn, 27 feet square, and sheded on three sides and
a floor full out with a shingle roof 8 years old and the
frame old in tolerable repair; one spring house, 8 feet
square; an orchard of about 240 apple trees 9 or 10 years
planted, and an old orchard of about 60 apple trees, old
and decaying; one peach orchard of about 50 trees; a small
meadow on the creek of about 6 acres and about 3 acres of
ditto on Cugates Run; cleared land divided into 7 fields
under tolerable fence; no more land must be cleared and no
green timber must be cut as there is sufficient old and
dead timber for repairs of building (and firewood) as the
quarters are rotten and repairs must be done and the
carpenters bill and nails accounted for. Signed by JOSIAS
HALL & JOHN CHAUNCY. Certified by JACOB FORWOOD.
FREDERICK COALE, aged 14 years (no birth date given) bound until
age 21 to GEORGE GALLION to learn the mercantile business,
with the usual freedom dues when age 21.
HESSE (a Mulatto girl) aged 11 years on April 21, 1796, was
bound until age 16 to SAMUEL FORWOOD to learn the house
hold business and to knit, spin and sew, and to receive the
usual freedom dues when she reaches age 16.
BEN (a Negro boy) aged 9 years in July, 1796, was bound to
SAMUEL FORWOOD until age 21 to learn the farm business and
to receive the customary freedom dues at age 21.
JOHN (a Negro boy) aged 7 years (no birth date given) bound
until age 21 to JAMES BOND to learn the farm business and
to read and write, with usual freedom dues at 21.
GILBERT MURPHY, aged 8 years on June 23, 1796, bound until age
21 to JAMES BOND to learn the farm business, and to read,
write and cipher as far as the rule of three, with the
customary freedom dues at age 21.
THOMAS SMITH and PACA SMITH came into Court and chose their
Uncle WILLIAM PACA as their guardian, with RICHARD DALLAM
and JOHN PHILEMON PACA approved as securities.
JOHN WOOD came into Court and chose MITCHEL STEWART as his
guardian. ROGER MATHEWS and MICHAEL MATHER, securities.
HUTSON WOOD came into Court and chose MICHAEL MATHER as his
guardian. ROGER MATHEWS and MITCHEL STEWART, security.
BILL (a Negro boy) aged 2 years and 4 months, bound until 21 to
THOMAS TAYLOR to learn the boy to work at some sort of
business or other, and to give him a suit of clothes when
he arrives at the age of 21.

JUNE COURT, 1796
Indenture, dated June 18, 1796, concerning BENJAMIN
    McCULLOH who was bound by his mother, MARY
    McCULLOH, to JOHN WILSON until age 21, stating
    said Benjamin was now four years and five months
    old, and said Wilson was to teach him the trade
    and art of weaving, and to read, write and cipher
    to the rule of three, and also to be kept in
    sufficient clothing, meat, washing and lodging
    suitable for an apprentice, and said Benjamin is
    to respect and be faithful to his master during
    this apprenticeship. Signed by JOHN WILSON and
    MARY McCULLOH (her mark), and witnessed by THOMAS
    BOND and NICHOLAS D. McCOMAS.
Indenture, dated August 11, 1796, concerning GEORGE
    LYTLE, JR. who was bound out with the consent of
    his father, GEORGE LYTLE, to JAMES JOHNSON to
    learn the trade of a house carpenter and joiner
    until January 19, 1801, at which time GEORGE
    LYTLE, JR. will be 21 years old. Said apprentice
    Lytle shall obey his master and shall do no
    damage to him willfully, nor play at cards, dice
    or any other unlawful game, nor contract
    matrimony during this term, nor absent himself
    without his master's leave, and in return the
    said Lytle shall receive training as agreed and
    be provided sufficient meat, drink, lodging and
    other necessaries fit an apprentice. Signed by
    GEORGE LYTLE, GEORGE LYTLE, JR., JAMES JOHNSON,
    and witnessed by THOMAS S. BOND and NICHOLAS D.
    McCOMAS. (Note: This indenture was dated August
    11, 1796, but it was recorded in the court
    records for June 14, 1796.(?)
AMOS BARNES to answer the complaint of MITCHEL
    STEWART. All appeared, and "a copy of inventory
    to the next court."
PEIRCE CREIGH and ROBERT HARRIS appeared in court as
    ordered and the case "stands till the next
    court."
ALEXANDER L. SMITH, ELIJAH DAVIS, SAMUEL GRIFFITH and
    FRANCES GARRETSON to show cause why they had not
    fully settled the estate of SAMUEL GRIFFITH, and
    to answer the complaint of MARTHA GRIFFITH.
    Appeared, and "the Court ordered the cost to be
    paid by the executors and to settle at next
    court. Appeal prayed and granted."
ELIZABETH CREITEN to answer the complaint of JOHN
    CREITEN.
HANNAH CAMPBELL to answer the complaint of WILLIAM
    SLADE. "Stands over to the next court."
DR. JOHN ARCHER "to testify, etc., etc. No Return."
Court appointed MARTIN TAYLOR GILBERT as guardian to
    LAWSON GORREL. Securities: THOMAS HALL and
    BENJAMIN PRESTON.
JOHN McKENLEY, aged 2 years (no birth date given)
    bound out until age 21 to CHARLES LEE to learn to
    read, write and cipher as far as the rule of
    three, with the customary freedom dues at 21.

AUGUST COURT, 1796
Court Justices present: JOHN RUMSEY and JAMES BOND.

CASSANDRA MORGAN, THOMAS CHEW, SAMUEL W. LEE and
JOSIAH LEE to answer the complaint of ELIZABETH
LEE, executrix of JAMES LEE.
Court appointed NICHOLAS HORNER as guardian to REBECCA
SMITH with JAMES DULEY and HENRY WETHERALL as
securities.
NICHOLAS BAKER, aged 18 years on September 15, 1796,
came into Court and chose WILLIAM LUCKEY as his
guardian, with EDWARD PRALL and RICHARD WEBSTER
as securities.
Court appointed GEN. JOHN CARLILE and COL. MICHAEL
GILBERT to audit and settle the accounts of HENRY
RUFF, SR. and MR. JOSIAS HALL, and to make return
to the next court.

SEPTEMBER COURT, 1796
JAMES WILSON, aged 4 years on August 9, 1796, bound
with the consent of his father to WILLIAM CHAPMAN
to have six months schooling and the apprentice
to have 3 days in every harvest, and to have all
necessary clothing and the customary freedom dues
at the expiration of his time. (Note: Record did
not indicate his trade/craft.)
ANN McCOMAS to answer the complaint of ALEXANDER
McCOMAS (of Aquila).
SARAH COOK to answer the complaint of the
representatives of ALICE SIMS.
NICHOLAS HORNER to answer the complaint of
representatives of JOHN DORNEY.
Court appointed JAMES DEBRULAR as guardian of SARAH
DEBRULAR and ELIZABETH GREENFIELD DEBRULAR, with
JOHN BAKER and WILLIAM DEBRULAR, JR. approved as
securities.
Court postponed the case of the Baylisses until next
court.
THOMAS JOHNSON, Esq. to testify the truth of his
knowledge in a matter between NATHAN BAYLIS and
SAMUEL BAYLIS.
WILLIAM HOLLIS, administrator of WILLIAM HOLLIS, to
show why he had not finally settled the estate of
the deceased, and also to answer the complaint of
GREENBERRY DORSEY.
GREENBERRY DORSEY, MARY FYE, SUSANNAH BROWN, and MARY
BROWN to testify to the truth of their knowledge
in a matter between AMOS BARNS and MITCHEL
STEWART.
SAMUEL EVEREST came into Court and chose JACOB
GREENFIELD as his guardian. Securties: GREENBERRY
and FRISBY DORSEY.
Court appointed WILLIAM SAVORY as guardian to EDWARD
MEAD, aged 14 in December, 1796, with JAMES
WETHERALL and SAMUEL RICKETTS, JR. approved as
securities.
Court appointed JACOB GREENFIELD as guardian to HENRY
AUSTIN EVANS. Securities: GREENBERRY DORSEY and
FRISBY DORSEY.

DECEMBER COURT, 1796
JOHN PENNEY, aged 17 years on December 25, 1796, bound
until age 21 to DANIEL McLOUGHLIN to learn the

61

occupation of bricklayer and to receive a suit of clothes at age 21.

SARAH JEMMESON, aged 6 years on August 25, 1796, bound until age 16 to SAMUEL COOK to learn to read and write and do household business, with customary freedom dues at 16.

LEE MORGAN came into Court and chose PARKER HALL LEE as his guardian. Securities: WILLIAM WILSON and THOMAS CHEW.

JOHN CAIN, aged 18 years on April 17, 1796, bound until age 21 to JOSHUA HUSBAND to learn the tanners and curriers trade and to receive 6 months schooling and if the said Husband shall die before the said time has expired, the said apprentice Cain shall serve no other person.

JAMES DEBRULAR came into Court and chose JAMES DULEY as his guardian. Securities: BENJAMIN CARROLL and...........

Court ordered an attachment be issued in MARTHA GRIFFITH's dispute with the executors of SAMUEL GRIFFITH.

ANN McCOMAS to answer the complaint of ALEXANDER McCOMAS (of Aquila).

SARAH COOK to show why she had not fully settled the estate of ROBERT COOK, and to answer the complaint of the representatives of ALSE (ALICE) SIMS.

WILLIAM HOLLIS to show why he had not fully settled the estate of WILLIAM HOLLIS, and to answer the complaint of GREENBERRY DORSEY.

Court ordered an attachment of AMOS BARNES for contempt, and also to answer the complaint of MITCHEL STEWART.

NATHANIEL BAYLIS to answer the complaint of SAMUEL BAYLIS.

MARCH COURT, 1797

Court Justices: JOHN RUMSEY, WILLIAM SMITH and JAMES BOND.

Court ordered an attachment of SARAH COOK for contempt, and to answer complaint of representatives of ALICE SIMS.

NATHANIEL BAYLIS to answer the complaint of SAMUEL BAYLIS.

Court attachment of ALEXANDER L. SMITH, ELIJAH DAVIS, SAMUEL GRIFFITH and FRANCES GARRETSON for contempt of court.

DAVID CLARK and WALTER BILLINGSLEY, JR. ordered to answer the complaint of JOHN LOVE.

HANNAH CAMPBELL to answer the complaint of WILLIAM SLADE. "Appeared and released. The Court will do nothing until the boy is of age."

ELIZABETH BAYLIS to answer complaint of PEREGRINE NOWLAND and JAMES DULEY.

ISAAC MITCHELL, aged 11 years (no birth date given) bound until age 21 to ISAAC WHITAKER to learn the farming business and to read, write and cipher to rule of 3.

BENJAMIN THOMAS, aged 12 years in November, 1797,
    bound until age 21 to THOMAS SAMSON to learn the
    weaver's trade and to read, write and cipher to
    the rule of 3.
Court appointed JOHN HOLLAND BARNEY as guardian to
    PHEBY STILES. Sec: RICHARD KRUSON and CAPT.
    GEORGE STILES.
Court appointed CAPT. GEORGE STILES as guardian to
    POLLY STILES (aged about 10 years), WILLIAM
    STILES (aged 8 years or so), and REBECCA STILES
    (aged 6 years) with RICHARD KRUSON and JOHN
    HOLLAND BARNEY as securities.
BENNETT MITCHELL came into Court and chose WILLIAM
    MITCHELL his guardian. Sec: PARKER MITCHELL
    and................
SAMUEL TUSSHE, aged 17 years or thereabouts (no birth
    date given) bound until age 21 to AMOS DAVIS to
    learn the cooper's trade, and to receive six
    months schooling.

APRIL COURT, 1797
SARAH COOK attached for contempt and to answer the
    complaint of the representatives of ALICE SIMS.
    (Did not appear)
JOHN COOK to return an inventory & other matters.
    Appeared.
Indenture, dated March 11, 1797, concerning GEORGE
    HUFF who was bound with the consent of his
    father, JOHN HUFF, to JACOB SWAN to learn his
    trade of wagon making, and the said apprentice
    shall obey his master, and not play cards or dice
    or any unlawful games, nor contract in matrimony,
    nor absent himself day or night from his master's
    service without permission, nor haunt taverns or
    playhouses or ale houses, or in any way cause
    harm to his master, and in return said apprentice
    Huff shall receive training for 4 years and 6
    months, plus learn to read, write and cipher as
    far as the rule of three, six months schooling,
    and a complete suit of clothes. Signed by JOHN
    HUFF (his mark), GEORGE HUFF (his mark) & JACOB
    SWAN. Wit: NICHOLAS D. McCOMAS, BENNETT BUSSEY.
GEORGE MICHAEL and MARTHA MICHAEL came into Court and
    chose ANN MICHAEL as their guardian. Approved
    securities were JOHN MICHAEL and ASHBERRY TAYLOR.
Court appointed ANN MICHAEL as guardian to AQUILA
    MICHAEL, ELIZABETH MICHAEL and HENRY MICHAEL.
    Approved securities were JOHN MICHAEL and
    ASHBERRY TAYLOR.
RACHEL MURRAY (a Negro girl) aged 8 years, bound until
    age 16 to JOHN MICHAEL to learn the household
    business, spinning, etc., with usual freedom dues
    at age 16.
HARRY (a Negro boy) aged 2 years on February 15, 1797,
    bound until age 21 to GILBERT JONES to learn
    farming business and to receive the usual freedom
    dues at age 21.

JAMES DEBRULAR came into Court and chose his Uncle
JAMES DEBRULAR as guardian. Approved securities
were NICHOLAS HORNER and WILLIAM YORK (of
George).
Court approved ROBERT AMOS, SR. and PEIRCE CREIGH as
counter securities for ELIZABETH BAYLIS,
administratrix of the goods and chattels of
AUGUSTINE BAYLIS, and to relieve PERRYGRINE
KNOWLAND and JAMES DULEY from that charge.

JUNE COURT, 1797
SARY COOK was attached for contempt, as well as to
answer the complaint of the representatives of
ALICE SIMS. Court appointed HENRY RICHARDSON and
SOLOMON PIRKINS to settle their matters.
JOHN COOK to show why he had returned an inventory of
the goods and chattels of JAMES COOK, and other
matters.
SAMUEL GOVER and ROBERT GOVER to show why they had not
returned an inventory for SAMUEL and PRISCILLA
GOVER.
PEIRCE CREIGH to answer the complaint of JAMES
MONTGOMERY.
REBECCA KNOWLAND, aged 11 years in July, 1797, bound
until age 16 to JACOB MICHAEL to learn to read,
write, sew, knit, spin, and do other household
business.
SARAH CLINE, aged 6 years in March, 1797, bound until
age 16 to JAMES FULTON to learn to read, write,
sew, knit, spin and do other household business.
Court continued the case of the Baylisses until next
court.
JAMES DEBRULAR, aged 17 years (no birth date given)
bound until age 21 to JAMES BILLINGSLEA to learn
the trade of cabinet maker, with usual freedom
dues at age 21.
Inventory of the goods and chattels, lands and
tenements of JAMES LEE MORGAN, legatee of WILLIAM
MORGAN, deceased, put into the hands of PARKER
HALL LEE, guardian of said legatee, as appraised
by JOHN FORWOOD, JR. and HENRY RUFF, JR. on March
1, 1797: Plantation appears to be in tenantable
repair as to fencing, but the house needs
considerable repair, a cellar ought to be dug out
and walled in, and lathing and plastering done
and filled in with cat and clay between it and
the weather board, and the second floor laid with
sufficient plank, but not at the expense of the
guardian (when done it should be kept in repair
by the guardian; also, the plantation contains a
small barn, kitchen, corn house, meat house and
stable; no land should be cleared except for some
under wood in a small place fronting the house,
and cut timber only for repairs and firewood; the
orchard has 60 old apple trees of which we
conceive no considerable advantage to the plow.
Plantation annual worth: 40 lbs. List of items: 1
cupboard, 10 cider hogsheads, 34 yards of blue
linen and cotton curtain stuff; 1 cotton & yarn
coverlet and 1 birdeyed coverlet; 1 bed quilt; 5
pairs of sheets; 2 pillow cases; 2 table cloths;
1 feather bed; 1 pair of blankets, 1 pair of
bedsteads; 6 pewter basins; 1 mare and blind

horse; 1 yoke of oxen; Negro London to serve 8
1/2 years; Negro Poll to serve 8 1/2 years; Negro
Robert, aged about 2 years, to serve until age
30. Verified by SAMUEL W. LEE on March 1, 1797.
Court appointed HENRY RICHARDS and SOLOMON PIRKINS to
audit and settle all matters in dispute between
SARAH COOK, administratrix of ROBERT COOK and
GEORGE ANDERSON who she administrates, and the
executors of ALICE SIMS.
SAMUEL GOVER, executor of PRISCILLA GOVER, to answer
the complaint of JAMES JOHNSON and show why the
estate of SAMUEL GOVER and PRISCILLA GOVER had
not been settled.
PEIRCE CREIGH to answer the complaint of JAMES
MONTGOMERY.

AUGUST COURT, 1797
JOHN COOK to show cause why he had not returned an
inventory of the goods and chattels of JAMES
COOK, deceased.
THOMAS CHEW to answer the complaint of ZACHEUS O.
BOND.
THOMAS McMULLEN, aged 4 years on September 17, 1797,
bound until age 21 to FORD BARNES (of William) to
learn the farming business, and read, write and
cipher up to 3.
WILLIAM (Negro boy aged 3 years) bound by Court to
WILLIAM WILSON (silversmith) to learn the farming
business and to read, with the customary freedom
dues at age 21.

OCTOBER COURT, 1797
Justices: JOHN RUMSEY, WILLIAM SMITH and JAMES BOND.
THOMAS CHEW to answer the complaint of ZACHEUS O.
BOND. Appeared in Court, nut no action taken.
CHARLOTTA (Negro girl aged about 6 years) bound by
Court to AQUILA NORRIS to learn to read, spin and
do other house hold business, with customary
freedom dues at age 16.
Court appointed MARTIN TAYLOR GILBERT as guardian to
LAWSON GORREL. Approved securities were CHARLES
GILBERT, SR. and CHARLES GILBERT, JR.
SARAH BRADY, aged 10 years, bound to INGREE THOMPSON
until age 16, to learn to read, write, sew, knit,
spin, and other household business, with usual
freedoms when 16.
Court ruled that THOMAS CHEW was to lay before the
Court the state of the settlement of WILLIAM
MORGAN's estate.

DECEMBER COURT, 1797
JOHN LONG, JR. to answer complaint of JOHN PETER COLIN
GINET and on refusal to delivery the property, an
attachment was issued. The Court ordered JOHN
LONG, JR. to deliver the property of CASSANDRA
GINET, late CASSANDRA SCOTT, into the hands of
PETER COLIN GINET, the guardian. JOHN RUTLEDGE
and JAMES POTEET were his securities.

SARAH COOK to show why she had not finally settled the
    estate of ROBERT COOK.
DAVID CANTLIN, "aged 15 years January, 1780"
    (questionable year), bound to JOHN MICHAEL until
    age 21 to learn to farm, and to read, write, and
    cipher to the rule of 3.

FEBRUARY COURT, 1798
JOHN LONG, JR. to answer for contempt against the
    Court, and to answer the complaint of PETER
    GINET.

MARCH COURT, 1798
NICHOLAS GASSAWAY to answer the complaint of MITCHEL
    STEWART.
SAMUEL CRAIL, aged 17 years on April 16, 1798, bound
    until age 21 to WILLIAM ATWELL to learn the
    cordwainer trade and to keep him in meat, drink,
    washing and lodging.

APRIL COURT, 1798
JOHN LONG, JR. was attached by the Court for contempt
    and for not delivering up the property of
    CASSANDRA GINET, late CASSANDRA SCOTT, to PETER
    GINET as ordered.
WILLIAM HITCHCOCK BARTON to show cause why he had not
    returned an inventory of the goods of ANN BARTON.
JOHN DORAN and PATRICK DORAN to answer the complaint
    of EDWARD DORAN and to show cause why the estate
    of MARGARET DORAN had not been finally settled.
GEORGE STILES to show cause why he had not returned an
    inventory of the goods and chattels of JOSEPH
    STILES.
CROUCH TALBY (TOLBY), aged 9 years on May 24, 1798,
    bound until age 21 to ISAIAH ROBERTS to learn the
    farming business, and to receive six month's
    schooling.
Court appointed CYRUS OSBORN as guardian of HENRY
    WARFIELD, aged 14 years in May, 1798, and
    approved BENJAMIN OSBORN and ALEXANDER McCOMAS as
    securities.
POLL (Negro girl child of Negro FAN) age 9 years on
    June 15, 1798, bound to MARY PIKE until age 16 to
    learn to read, etc., and to receive the usual
    freedom dues at age 16.
JOHN RYLERY, aged 15 years on November 27, 1797, bound
    until age 21 to JOHN REARDON to learn to read,
    write and cipher to the rule of 3, and usual
    freedom dues at 21.

JUNE COURT, 1798
JOHN DORAN and PATRICK DORAN to show cause why the
    estate of MARGARET DORAN has not been fully
    settled and to answer the complaint of EDWARD
    DORAN.
WILLIAM HITCHCOCK BARTON to show why he had not
    returned an inventory of the goods and chattels
    of ANN BARTON, of which he is administrator.

DAVID CLARK and WALTER BILLINGSLEY, JR. to answer
    complaint of JACOB LOVE and to show cause why the
    estate of JOHN LOVE had not been finally settled.
WATT (Mulatto boy aged 15 years) bound until age 21 to
    AQUILA MITCHELL to learn the farming business and
    to receive the customary freedom dues at age 16.
Court appoints AQUILA MITCHELL guardian to WINSTON
    MITCHELL. Securities were THOMAS JOHNSON and
    WILLIAM MITCHELL.
JAMES HALL, aged 15 years and 6 months, bound until
    age 21 to JAMES JOHNSON to learn the carpenter's
    trade, and to receive the customary freedom dues
    at age 21.
HARRIOTT (Negro girl supposed to be age 7 years) bound
    until age 16 to JAMES AMOS to learn to read and
    do household business, with customary freedom
    dues at age 16.
EDWARD McCOMAS, aged 13 years in March, 1798, bound
    until age 21 to ALEXANDER McCOMAS to learn the
    blacksmith's trade, and to read, write and cipher
    to rule of three, and to receive the customary
    freedom dues at age 21.

JULY COURT, 1798, ADJOURNED TO AUGUST, 1798
Court Justices: JOHN RUMSEY, WILLIAM SMITH and JAMES
    BOND.
Indenture, dated August 4, 1798, concerning GEORGE
    HEARN who bound himself to ROBERT MOORE (miller)
    to be taught his trade for a term to expire three
    years next Christmas. Said Hearn will faithfully
    serve his master and keep his secrets, and not
    cause any harm to his master nor misbehave
    towards him, and in return said Moore will teach
    him the miller's trade, and keep said Hearn in
    meat, drink, washing and lodging, also find him
    three shirts, two pair of trousers, two pair of
    shoes, one hat, one coat jacket and overalls of
    cloth, one pair of cotton stocking, one neck and
    one pocket handkerchief every year during said
    term, and one suit of gingham or nonkeen (?), and
    at the completion of said term he will receive
    one hat, one pair of shoes and stockings, one
    coat jacket and breeches of cloth, one neck and
    one pocket handkerchief and knee buckles and
    sleeve buttons and five pounds in cash. Signed by
    GEORGE HEARN and ROBERT MOORE. Taken before JOHN
    WESTON and JOHN RUMSEY.
GEORGE STILES had not returned an inventory of the
    goods of JOSEPH STILES and passed a final
    account. The Court issued an attachment for his
    contempt of court and he finally appeared. His
    inventory was taken and recorded.
WALTER BILLINGSLEY, JR. (not cited) and DAVID CLARK
    (cited) to show cause why the estate of JOHN LOVE
    had not been finally settled and also to answer
    the complaint of JACOB LOVE. DAVID CLARK
    appeared in court as ordered.
JOHN DORAN (cited) and PATRICK DORAN (not cited) to
    show why the estate of MARGARET DORAN had not

been finally settled, and to answer the complaint of EDWARD DORAN.

WILLIAM HITCHCOCK BARTON (cited) to show why he had not returned an inventory of the goods and chattels of ANN BARTON as administrator. Appeared in court as ordered.

ROBERT MORGAN (cited) to show why he had not finally settled the estate of EDWARD MORGAN and to answer the complaint of DIXSON SLADE. Appeared in court as ordered.

Court ordered that HENRY BOWMAN be released from his charge of his apprentice GILBERT MURPHY with the consent of his mother who chooses it.

OCTOBER COURT, 1798 SET, BUT ADJOURNED UNTIL DECEMBER, 1798.

NO COURTS WERE HELD IN DECEMBER, 1798, OR IN FEBRUARY, 1799.

APRIL COURT, 1799

THOMAS ELLIOTT to show why the estate of THOMAS ELLIOTT had not been finally settled, and to answer the complaint of JOHN FORWOOD, SR.

ANN ELLIOTT to testify the truth of her knowledge in a matter between JOHN FORWOOD and THOMAS ELLIOTT.

HANNAH BURNETT to answer complaint of WILLIAM D. HAWKINS.

ELIZABETH CRETIN to show why the estate of JOHN CRETIN had not been finally settled, and to answer the complaint of PATRICK CRETIN.

GEORGE STILES to show why the estate of JOSEPH STILES had not been finally settled.

DAVID CLARK and WALTER BILLINGSLEY, JR. to show cause why the estate of JOHN LOVE had not been finally settled, and also to answer the complaint of JACOB LOVE.

JOHN DORAN and PATRICK DORAN to show cause why the estate of MARGARET DORAN had not been finally settled, and also to answer the complaint of EDWARD DORAN.

WILLIAM PACA (of Aquila) came into Court and chose RICHARD DALLAM his guardian. Approved securities were JOSIAS WILLIAM DALLAM and DR. PHILIP HENDERSON.

ANN PACA came into Court and chose JOSIAS WILLIAM DALLAM as her guardian. Approved securities were RICHARD DALLAM and WILLIAM SMITH, Esq.

BENJAMIN BAYLIS came into Court and chose JAMES STEPHENSON as his guardian. Approved securities were JOHN HAMBLETON and THOMAS JEFFERY.

Court appointed SAMUEL BAYLIS as guardian of MARY BAYLIS, JAMES BAYLIS and NATHANIEL BAYLIS. Approved securities were BENJAMIN SILVER and ROBERT NISBIT.

MAY COURT, 1799

MICHAEL HENDRICK, aged 16 years on October 29, 1799, bound until age 21 to PARKER GILBERT, JR. to learn to read, write and cipher to the rule of

three, and to learn the taylor's trade, with usual
   freedom dues when age 21.
Court appointed JOSIAS WILLIAM DALLAM as guardian of
   FRANCIS DALLAM PACA. Approved securities were
   RICHARD DALLAM and WILLIAM SMITH, Esq.

JUNE COURT, 1799
DAVID CLARK and WALTER BILLINSGLEY, JR. to show cause
   why the estate of JOHN LOVE had not been finally
   settled, and answer the complaint of JACOB LOVE.
   (Nothing done.)
THOMAS ELLIOTT to show cause why the estate of THOMAS
   ELLIOTT, SR. had not been finally settled, and
   answer the complaint of JOHN FORWOOD, SR.
   (Nothing done.)
ANN ELLIOTT to testify the truth of her knowledge in a
   matter between JOHN FORWOOD and THOMAS ELLIOTT.
   (Did not appear in court.)
HANNAH BURNETT to answer complaint of WILLIAM D.
   HAWKINS. (Case discharged, with plaintiff paying
   the costs.)
ELIZABETH CRETIN to show cause why the estate of JOHN
   CRETIN had not been finally settled, and to
   answer complaint of PATRICK CRETIN. (Did not
   appear.)
JOHN DORAN and PATRICK DORAN to show cause why the
   estate of MARGARET DORAN had not been finally
   settled, and answer the complaint of EDWARD
   DORAN.   (Did not appear.)
ARCHABALD ROBINSON and THOMAS BARTON to show cause why
   the estate of JAMES BARTON had not been finally
   settled, and to answer complaint of THOMAS
   JOHNSON and JAMES BARTON. (Appeared; nothing
   done.)
RICHARD BULL to answer the complaint of WILLIAM
   HENDRICKSON. (His letters de bonis non on JOHN
   HENDRICKSON's estate were revoked by the Court.)
GEORGE STILES to show cause why the estate of JOSEPH
   STILES had not been finally settled.
WILLIAM SMITHSON (of Daniel) came into Court and chose
   WILLIAM SMITHSON, Esq., as his guardian.
   Approved securities were JOHN GUYTON and HENRY
   DORSEY.
Court directed BENJAMIN PRITCHARD to advertise 6
   months from this date in Yount and Brown's for
   three weeks for the creditors of the estate of
   BENJAMIN BRUSEBANKS to bring in their claims
   agreeable to Act of Assembly.
Court appointed SARAH WILSON as guardian to her sons,
   namely PETER WILSON, aged 8 years on October 22,
   1798, and THOMAS WILSON aged 7 years in January,
   1799, and, NATHAN WILSON, aged 5 years in
   December, 1798. Approved securities were PETER
   WILSON and JOHN WILSON.
Court bound REASON ROSE, formerly bound to WILLIAM
   MITCHELL, now to PHILLIP BENNETT, to learn the
   shoemaker's trade and to read, write and cipher
   as far as the rule of 3.
Court appointed JANES LUCKIE as guardian of HUGH
   FINLEY LUCKIE and WILLIAM ANNEN LUCKIE. She
   offered EDWARD PRALL and JAMES BELL as
   securities. Court approved.

WILLIAM PACA (of Aquila) came into Court and chose
    RICHARD DALLAM (of William) as his guardian.
    PHILIP HENDERSON and JOSIAS WILLIAM DALLAM were
    approved as securities.
CHARLES GILBERT, aged 16 years, came into Court and
    chose THOMAS HALL as his guardian. WILLIAM HALL
    and JOHN HALL were approved as securities.
Court appointed THOMAS HALL as guardian of CLEMMENCY
    HUGHES GILBERT, aged 10 years, ELIZABETH GILBERT,
    aged 8 years and WILLIAM PRESBURY GILBERT, aged 6
    years. Court approved WILLIAM HALL and JOHN HALL
    as securities.
Court directed THOMAS JEFFERY and JAMES STEPHENSON,
    admins. of the estate of NATHANIEL BAYLIS, to
    advertise for six months from this date in Yount
    and Brown's paper three weeks for the creditors
    to bring in their claims.
JOE DURHAM came into Court and chose THOMAS DURHAM as
    his guardian. Securities: LOYD DURHAM and
    ALEXANDER YOUNG.

AUGUST COURT, 1799
DAVID CLARK and WALTER BILLINGSLEY, JR. to show cause
    why the estate of JOHN LOVE had not been finally
    settled, and also to answer the complaint of
    JACOB LOVE. (They appeared, but case was
    postponed until next court.)
THOMAS ELLIOTT to show why the estate of THOMAS
    ELLIOTT had not been finally settled, and to
    answer the complaint of JOHN FORWOOD, SR.
    (Appeared.)
ANN ELLIOTT to testify the truth of their knowledge in
    a matter between THOMAS ELLIOTT and JOHN FORWOOD,
    SR. (Did not appear.)
ELIZABETH CRETIN to show why the estate of JOHN CRETIN
    had not been finally settled, and to answer the
    complaint of PATRICK CRETIN. (Did not appear.)
JOHN DORAN and PATRICK DORAN to show why the estate of
    MARGARET DORAN had not been finally settled, and
    to answer the complaint of EDWARD DORAN.
RICHARD COALE to answer the complaint of SARAH WILSON
    and PETER WILSON, executors of THOMAS WILSON,
    deceased.
JOHN WOOD to show why he had not returned an inventory
    of the goods and chattels of EZEKIEL BAYLEY,
    deceased.
JAMES DEBRULAR to answer the complaint of JOHN GROVES.
SAMUEL BAYLIS, administrator of NATHANIEL BAYLIS, to
    answer the complaint of LEMUEL KENLEY.
GEORGE STILES to show why the estate of JOSEPH STILES
    had not been finally settled.
JOHN MILLAR, aged 13 years, bound until age 21 to
    CROASDEL WARNER to learn the wagon wheelwright's
    trade, and to read, write and cipher as far as
    the rule of three.
Court appointed CATHARINE BROWNLEY as guardian to
    CATHARINE BROWNLEY (minor), JAMES BROWNLEY and
    JOHN BROWNLEY. Securities were THOMAS JEFFERY and
    DR. JOHN ARCHER.

SARAH (Negro girl aged 6 years on October 23, 1799)
    bound to SAMUEL McCONNEL until age 16, to learn
    to read, sew and spin and do other household
    business, and to receive the usual freedom dues
    at age 16.

OCTOBER COURT, 1799
Justices: WILLIAM SMITH, JAMES BOND and JOHN RUMSEY.
DAVID CLARK and WALTER BILLINGSLEY, JR. to show cause
    why the estate of JOHN LOVE had not been finally
    settled, and to answer the complaint of JACOB
    LOVE.
THOMAS ELLIOTT to show why the estate of THOMAS
    ELLIOTT had not been finally settled, and to
    answer the complaint of JOHN FORWOOD, SR.
ANN ELLIOTT to testify the truth of her knowledge in a
    matter between THOMAS ELLIOTT and JOHN FORWOOD,
    SR.
Attachment issued for JOHN DORAN and PATRICK DORAN to
    show why the estate of MARGARET DORAN had not
    been finally settled, and to answer the complaint
    of EDWARD DORAN.
RICHARD COALE to answer complaint of PETER and SARAH
    WILSON.
JAMES DEBRULAR to answer complaint of JOHN GRAVES
    (GROVES?).
GEORGE STILES to show cause why he had not finally
    settled the estate of JOSEPH STILES.
ARCHABALD ROBINSON to answer the complaint of THOMAS
    JOHNSON and FRANCES CRAWFORD.
Court ordered CORDELIA BAKER, administratrix of JOHN
    BAKER, to sell the property of the deceased at
    public auction, and to give thirty days notice
    and six month's credit, with good security.
LINDEY (Negro girl aged 2 years on August 1, 1799)
    bound to WILLIAM CREAL until age 16 to learn to
    read, spin, knit and other household business,
    with freedom dues at 16.
Court ordered the sale of the personal property of
    JOHN HANSON, deceased, at public auction by JONAS
    COURTNEY, executor (negroes excepted), giving
    thirty days notice and six month's credit, with
    good security.
AARON DILLON, aged 11 years on April 1, 1799, bound
    until age 21 to WILLIAM MICHAEL to learn the
    taylor's trade and to read, write and cipher as
    far as the rule of 3.
(Entry about RICHARD CROESON unclear and illegibly
    written.)
HENRY SUTTO, "aged 9 years aged 11 years" (?) on
    January 22, 1800, bound until age 21 to ALEXANDER
    McCOMAS to learn the farming business with the
    usual freedom dues at 21.
Court ordered REBECCA GILES to advertise in Yount &
    Brown's requesting the creditor's of THOMAS GILES
    to bring in their claims properly authenticated.
MOSAS (MOSNAS?), a Negro boy aged 13 years on February
    10, 1800, bound until age 21 to JONAS COURTNEY to
    learn the carpenter's trade with the usual
    freedoms due at 21.

Court appointed DAVID CRAIN guardian of SEMELIA
LANCASTER. Securities were GEROGE CHAUNCY, JR.
and JOSIAH MATHERS.
Court ordered THOMAS JEFFREY, administrator of RALPH
SMITH, to give notice in Yount and Brown's papers
for the creditors to exhibit their claims against
said Smith.
Court ordered GEORGE CHAUNCY, SR. and CLARK HOLLIS to
value the real estate of SEMELIA LANCASTER and
their return.
Court appointed MAJ. SAMUEL SMITH and THOMAS JEFFREY
to estimate the yearly value of the real estate
of JOSEPH BROWNLEY and make their return.
Court ordered an attachment against the lands,
tenements, goods and chattels of GEORGE STILES,
executor of JOSEPH STILES, to compel his
appearance and abide by future Court orders.
(sequestration issue) JOHN MONTGOMERY, attorney
in behalf of GEORGE STILES, executor of JOSEPH
STILES, prayed an appeal from this order to the
General Court and it was granted. Record noted
that GEORGE STILES was not present and did not
appear on citation.
HUTCHEN PIKE to answer the complaint of JAMES GALLION
and REBECCA STALLIONS. Appeared in court, and
REBECCA STALLIONS ordered to give counter
security.
CAPT. ROGER BOYCE to show cause why he had not
returned an inventory of the goods and chattels
of ALEXANDER COWAN and pass a final account, and
to answer the complaint of BOYCE COWAN and AQUILA
HALL. (Did not appear.)
ARCHABALD ROBINSON to show cause why the estate of
JAMES BARTON has not been finally settled, and to
answer the complaint of THOMAS JOHNSON and
FRANCES CRAWFORD.
Court ordered attachment of RICHARD COALE for contempt
and to answer complaint of PETER WILSON and SARAH
WILSON.
SAMUEL WEBB to show cause why the estate of SAMUEL
WEBB had not been finally settled, and to answer
the complaint of THOMAS HALL. ("Was unwell and
not able to attend.")

JANUARY COURT, 1800
Court ordered the sale of the goods and chattels of
GEDION DENISON be sold at public auction (vendue)
and that proper three week notice be given in the
public papers.
Court ordered a citation be issued for NICHOLAS
McCOMAS.
Court ordered DAVID CLENDENIN, administrator of
BENJAMIN ADAMS, to advertise in Yount and Brown's
papers for the creditors to bring in the claims
to receive dividends.
JOHN BARNES, aged 17 years in March, 1800, bound until
age 21 to JAMES BILLINGSLEA to learn the cabinet
maker's trade with the customary freedom dues at
age 21.

EPHRAIM COLLERAL, aged 12 years on May 18, 1800, bound
until age 21 to JAMES BILLINGSLEA to learn to
read, write and cipher as far as rule of 3, with
usual freedoms at 21.
Court revoked the Letters of Administration granted to
REBECCA STALLIONS and AQUILA PIKE since she did
not give counter security. Court then issued
letters to HUTCHEN PIKE and JAMES GALLION.
HANNAH BURNET, administrator of...........BURNET (no
first name given), ordered to advertise in Yount
and Brown's papers for creditors to bring in
their claims.

FEBRUARY COURT, 1800
Court Justices: JOHN RUMSEY, WILLIAM SMITH and JAMES
BOND.
Court ordered attachment of ARCHABALD ROBINSON for
contempt, and to show why the estate of JAMES
BARTON had not been finally settled, and to
answer the complaint of THOMAS JOHNSON and
FRANCES CRAWFORD. (Still did not appear.)
CAPT. ROGER BOYCE to show why he had not returned an
inventory of the goods and chattels of ALEXANDER
COWAN and pass a final account, and to answer
complaint of AQUILA HALL and BOYCE COWAN.
(Attachment ordered.)
ROGER MATHEWS to show why he had not returned an
inventory of the goods and chattels of BENNET
MATHEWS and LEVEN MATHEWS, and pass a final
account, and to answer the complaint of JAMES
BILLINGSLEA. (Case laid over.)
NICHOLAS McCOMAS to show why he had not exhibited the
last of his father ALEXANDER McCOMAS, deceased.
(Probably meant last will and testament) Case
laid over. (It appears that AQUILA HALL was
defendant's attorney.)
SAMUEL WEBB to show why the estate of SAMUEL WEBB had
not been finally settled, and to answer the
complaint of THOMAS HALL. (Case laid over.)
GARRET GARRETSON to answer the complaint of JOHN
COUSINS.
Court appointed MAJ. SAMUEL SMITH and THOMAS COURTNEY
to estimate the yearly value of the real estate
of CHARLES GILBERT, deceased, and make their
return in next court.
GARRET BROWN, aged 10 years on January 26, 1800, bound
until age 21 to JOHN MITCHELL to learn to read,
write and cipher as far as the rule of three and
to learn to use carpenter's tools, with customary
freedom dues at 21.
Court appointed MAJ. SAMUEL SMITH and CAPT. WILLIAM
SMITH to divide the negroes belonging to the
estate of WILLIAM LUCKEY, deceased, among his
representatives.
Court appointed MAJ. SAMUEL SMITH and THOMAS JEFFERY
to divide the negroes, the late property of
JOSEPH BROWNLEY, deceased, among his
representatives.
Court ordered the sale of the negroes belonging to
estate of BENJAMIN BRUSEBANKS, deceased, and give
proper notice in the public papers previous to
the sale.

Court appointed RICHARD DALLAM to take the property of
GEORGE STILES, as returned and scheduled by the
Sheriff of Baltimore County, into his possession.
Court appointed JOHN STREET in the room of JOHN COX to
divide the estate of MARGARET DORAN, deceased,
among her representatives.
EDWARD EVINS, aged 14 years on June 6, 1800, bound
until age 21 to AMOS OSBORN to learn the
millwright's trade, and to read, write and cipher
as far as the rule of three, with customary
freedom dues at age 21.
Court revoked the Letters of Administration granted to
JOHN BOND on the estate of RALPH BOND and the
administration was committed to DENNIS BOND and
NICHOLAS M. BOSLEY.
Court appointed SAMUEL SMITH and THOMAS JEFFERY to
divide the personal estate of JOSEPH BROWNLEY,
deceased, among his representatives.
Court appointed WILLIAM MITCHELL and MARTHA MITCHELL
as the guardians of HARRIOTT MITCHELL, aged 10
years in March, 1800, and JAMES MITCHELL, aged 6
years on November 15, 1799, and AQUILA MITCHELL,
aged 3 years on December 3, 1799. Approved
securities were PARKER MITCHELL and GREGORY
BARNES, JR.

APRIL COURT, 1800
GARRETT GARRETSON to answer the complaint of JOHN
COUSINS.
Court appointed ELIZABETH WARD as guardian of ANN
WARD, and THOMAS JOHNSON and ROBERT BRIARLY were
securities.
Court appointed BERNARD JOHNSON (of Bernard) as
guardian to JAMES WARD and WILLIAM WARD.
Approved securities were WILLIAM PYLE and WILLIAM
McMATH.
RICHARD WARD, aged 17 years in November, 1800, bound
until age 21 to WILLIAM MITCHELL to learn the
shoemaker trade and to receive six month's
schooling, with customary freedom dues at age 21.
AQUILLA STALLIONS, aged 8 years in March, 1800, bound
until age 21 to JEHUE WATLEY to learn the
bricklayer and stone mason trade, and to read,
write and cipher as far as the rule of 3, with
customary freedom dues at 21.

(EDITOR'S NOTE: The original book containing the
records of the Harford County Orphan Court
Proceedings, 1778-1800, contains the foregoing
text from pages 1 through 162. It is then
followed by blank pages and a partial index from
pages 163 through 261. It then has more proceeds
(as follows) from pages 262 through 289, and ends
with the remaining partial index. The original
book measures approximately 7 1/2" by 16 1/2"
and, as of 1990, it is in the office of the
Register of Wills in Bel Air, MD.)

Indenture, dated September 9, 1799, involving WILLIAM
WILLIAMS (of John) of Havre de Grace who put
himself by his own free will and with the
consent of his father, JOHN WILLIAMS, SR., to be

a carpenter's apprentice to PLATT WHITAKER for 4
years beginning November 2, 1799 and during that
time he is to obey his master, etc., and receive
training, housing, etc. in return. Signed by
PLATT WHITAKER, WILLIAM WILLIAMS, JOHN WILLIAMS,
in presence of ROBERT HOLLIDAY and W. HANDS, and
verified by JOHN H. BARNEY and ALEXANDER ROGERS,
Sept. 9, 1799.

Indenture, dated August 24, 1799, involving BARACK
    WILLIAMS of Havre de Grace who put himself by his
    own free will to be a baker's apprentice to JOHN
    MYERS for 8 years, and during that time he is to
    obey his master, etc., and receive training,
    clothing, etc. in return. Signed by JOHN MYERS,
    BARACK WILLIAMS and WILLIAM WILLIAMS, in presence
    of W. HANDS, and verified by JOHN H. BARNEY and
    ALEXANDER ROGERS, August 24, 1799.

Indenture, dated August 24, 1799, involving BENNETT
    WILLIAMS of Havre de Grace who put himself by his
    own free will and with the consent of his father,
    WILLIAM WILLIAMS, to be a taylor's apprentice to
    JOHN PORTER for 6 years, and during that time he
    is to obey his master, etc., and receive
    training, clothing, etc. in return. Signed by
    JOHN PORTER, BENNETT WILLIAMS and WILLIAM
    WILLIAMS, in presence of W. HANDS, and verified
    by JOHN H. BARNEY and ALEXANDER ROGERS, August
    24, 1799.

Indenture, dated January 29, 1799, involving JOHN
    BENSON.... (rest of page is blank)

Indenture, dated February 27, 1800, involving PATRICK
    TODD who put his daughter NANCY TODD as an
    apprentice to JONAS BARECROFT until she arrives
    at age 16, which will be on September 20, 1808,
    to learn to read the Bible and to write and to
    receive sufficent clothing, etc., and at the end
    of this apprenticeship she is to receive a good
    bonnet, a callico gownd (?) and full suit of
    clothes, and said JONAS BARECROFT and wife are to
    also teach her to spin, sew, knit and do other
    such work. Signed by PATRICK TODD and JONAS
    BARECROFT, in the presence of JESSE GARRETT and
    THOMAS BOND, as verified by said JESSE GARRETT
    and THOMAS BOND, Feb. 27, 1800.

Indenture, dated January 29, 1799, involving JOHN
    BENSON who bound himself to EDWARD TIMMONS to be
    taught to farm or to be a mariner or any other
    trade or occupation that said Timmons shall carry
    on with him, and Benson shall obey his master,
    etc. and receive training, etc. in return. Signed
    by EDWARD TIMMONS and JOHN BENSON (his mark), in
    presence of JOHN RUMSEY and JOHN WESTON.

Justices WILLIAM SMITHSON and JAMES BOND bound SARAH
    CARROLL (aged about 14 years last July) to JOHN
    CRUIT until she reaches age 16 to learn to read,

during which time she will receive sufficient accommodations and then receive the usual freedoms at 16. Signed on September 21, 1798.

Indenture, dated November 18, 1799, involving JAMES PACA, son of SARAH THOMAS, who put himself by his own free will and the consent of his mother, to be a shoemaker's apprentice to CHRISTIAN WASKEY of Abingdon Town for 3 years and 4 months, and to be sent to school during the last 6 months of that time, and Paca shall obey his master, etc. and will receive training, etc. in return. Signed by JAMES PACA (his mark) and CHRISTIAN WASKEY, in the presence of THOMAS BOND and WILLIAM SMITH.

Indenture, dated November 14, 1799, involving JUDY, a free Negro, who bound her son ABRAM to JOHN CORD of Joppa as an apprentice to learn to be a shoemaker until age 21, and said Abram shall obey his master, etc. and receive training, etc. with the usual freedoms allowed by law. Signed by JOHN CORD and free Negro JUDITH (her mark), in the presence of JOHN RUMSEY and JOHN WESTON.

Indenture, dated November 2, 1798, involving JOHN SIVERS, son of ELIZABETH TATE, who was bound by his own free will and the consent of his mother to JOSEPH PRIGG to be a cordwainer's apprentice until March 30, 1802 or until he reaches age 21, and he is to obey his master, etc., and receive training, etc. in return. Signed by JOHN SIVERS, ELIZABETH TATE (her mark) and JOSEPH PRIGG in presence of JOHN BARKLEY and SIMON NEVILL. Verified by JOHN BARCLAY and ROBERT MORGAN.

Indenture, dated March 3, 1798, between GABRIEL CHRISTIE and SAMUEL JAY, merchants, trading under the firm of Samuel Jay and Company in the town of Havre de Grace, MD, and SAMUEL HUGHES MACNABB, son of JOHN MACNABB, who bound himself to them as an apprentice in mercantile business matters. Said apprentice shall not absent himself from this employment without his masters' permission first, and for every day or hour he absents himself without such leave obtained, he will serve four days or four hours after the expiration of the apprenticeship term, said term to end October 17, 1803 (five years, 8 months and 17 days in full), and if any of the parties fail to meet their obligation in this indenture, then the other party shall receive $270 in payment from the party who failed to observe and perform this indenture. Signed by SAMUEL HUGHES MACNABB, JOHN MACNABB, and SAMUEL JAY for himself and GABRIEL CHRISTIE. Witness: ROGER BOYCE.

Indenture, dated June 16, 1798, involving ELENOR SCHOFIELD, daughter of JOHN SCHOFIELD, who bound herself by her own free will and the consent of her father to JOHN CROSSON to learn to spin,

knit, sew and do other house work for a term of 6
years and 10 months. Said Elenor shall obey her
master and receive said training and 9 months
schooling. Signed: JOHN CROSSON, ELENOR SCHOFIELD
(her mark), and JOHN SCHOFIELD, in the presence
of JOHN BARCLAY and JOHN STREET.

Statement signed by Justices WILLIAM SMITH and THOMAS
BOND on July 8, 1799, that a Negro woman named
LIEU (?) had some time before her death put her
two sons ABRAHAM and JOHN to HERMAN STUMP to
serve him until age 21. Abraham is judged this
date to be 11 years old and John 8 years old.
They were bound by the Court to said Stump until
age 21 to learn husbandry, other plantation work,
and to wait and tend in the house.

On April 19, 1797, Justice WILLIAM SMITH along with
GODFREY WATERS, appointed guardian for JOHN RUFF,
a child of HENRY RUFF, deceased, and in behalf of
the guardian for the other children of HENRY
RUFF, together with JOHN MOORES and JOHN CARTER,
two persons of good repute and well skilled in
building and plantation affairs and having no
interest in this estate, entered upon the lands
of HENRY RUFF, deceased, and valued the property
as follows: (1) Dwelling house and all outhouses
with the tanyard in Harford Town at 62 pounds, 1
sh. and 3 pence per year; dwelling house and
kitchen in midling repair; one small framed meat-
house, old and bad repair; one small log henhouse
indifferent; a garden in bad repair; one small
framed leather house in good repair; one log corn
house indifferent; old framed stable indifferent;
stone currying shop midling good; log bark house
indifferent; log dwelling house very good; small
blacksmith shop good; small log house very bad; a
beam house very bad; the meadows fenced in
midling repair; (2) Stiles, 50 acre lot out of
town, the liberty to maul rails to fence in a
half acre for a garden and likewise to build   a
chimney in the dwelling house on said lot; 3
acres under bad fence; 7 acres of old field, no
fence around it; nothing but dead wood to be used
for firewood; valued at 6 pounds per year; (3)
Farm on Winters Run, 40 acres under midling good
fence and now in cultivation; 10 acres of old
field under no fence; 21 acres in woodland very
indifferently timbered; valued at 16 pounds per
year; granted privilege to   build a 20 feet by 18
feet house with a stone chimney and two floors to
be build out of timber cut elsewhere and paid for
out of rent (30 pounds). Signed by JOHN MOORES
and JOHN CARTER, and verified by WILLIAM SMITH.

Indenture, dated December 28, 1797, involving LUCAS
GILLIAM, son of LUCAS GILLIAM, who voluntarily
bound himself, with the consent of his father, as
apprentice to ISAAC PENNINGTON to learn the art
of "flower barrel making". Said Gilliam shall

77

obey his master, etc. and receive in return this training and 12 months' schooling. Signed by LUCAS GILLIAM (his mark), LUCAS GILLIAM, and ISAAC PENNINGTON. Wit: JOHN WESTON and JOHN RUMSEY, Justices.

Indenture, dated March 17, 1798, involving HENRIETTA SCHOFIELD, daughter of JOHN SCHOFIELD, who voluntarily bound herself, with the consent of her father, as an apprentice to NICHOLAS COOPER to learn to spin, knit, sew and do other house work for the term of four years and ten months. Said Schofield shall obey her master, etc., and receive said training and 5 months' schooling in return. Signed By HENRIETTA (HENNERITTA) SCHOFIELD, JOHN SCHOFIELD, and NICHOLAS COOPER in the presence of JOHN BARCLAY and JOHN STREET.

Indenture, dated March 19, 1798, involving WILLIAM PRESBURY SMITH (son of Josiah Smith), who will be 18 years old on September 20th, who was put by his father under the apprenticeship of PARKER GILBERT to learn the taylor's trade until he reaches age 21. Said Smith shall obey his master, etc. and receive two months' schooling and a full suit of new apparel. Said apprenticeship was so ordered by JACOB FORWOOD and THOMAS S. BOND, Justices.

Indenture, dated February 14, 1798, involving WILLIAM ANDERSON who was bound with the consent of his mother to THOMAS MITCHELL as an apprentice for twelve years to learn farming and the distilling of grain into spirits. Said Anderson shall obey his master at all times, shall not commit fornication, shall not play card games or haunt taverns or ale houses, etc., and in return shall receive said training and learn to read the Bible, to write legibly, and to do arithmetic as far as the five common rules or the rule of three. At the term's end, said Anderson shall receive a new suit of clothes from head to foot equal to the amount of 7 pounds. Signed by WILLIAM ANDERSON (his mark) and THOMAS MITCHELL, in the presence of JOHN BARCLAY and ROBERT MORGAN.

On January 14, 1799, Court Justice JACOB NORRIS ordered GEORGE CHAUNCEY and AMOS HOLLIS to attend the house of CYRUS OSBORN on January 19, 1799 and proceed from there with the said Osborn to the farm where HENRY WARFIELD resided and then value the farm's worth and make any suggestions for improvements. It was done, and the value was placed at 17 pounds, 10 shillings per year, and they suggested that a new corn house and and a new kitchen be built and paid for out of the annual rent.

MARY SMITHSON stated that she had received on January 28, 1800, of her son NATHANIEL SMITHSON, executor of her deceased husband THOMAS SMITHSON, the full amount or compensation of her estate agreeable to the inventory willed to her by her husband. (Signed with her mark.)

BENJAMIN SMITHSON stated he had received on February 3, 1800 of NATHANIEL SMITHSON, the executor of his (Benjamin's) grandfather THOMAS SMITHSON, the full amount of his estate

agreeable to the inventory as willed to him by his
grandfather. Signed by BENJAMIN SMITHSON. Witnessed by
EDWARD HAMBLETON, JR.

Report by JOHN LEE GIBSON and THOMAS GILES who were ordered to
value the real estate of WILLIAM SMITH (Bayside) on January
29, 1798: 180 acre farm, of which 100 acres is cleared
land, under very bad fence; one log dwelling house, 38 feet
by 24 feet, one story high, covered with oak shingles in
bad repair; one log dwelling house, two stories high, 28
feet by 22 feet, covered with cedar shingles in bad repair;
one kitchen, 21 feet by 22 feet in bad repair; one stone
meat house, 20 feet by 18 feet in good repair; one ash and
oven house, 14 feet by 12 feet in bad repair; one stove and
carriage house framed and clapboarded, 22 1/2 feet by 18
feet in good repair; one hen house, 16 feet by 15 feet, in
bad repair; one stone spring house, 10 feet by 12 feet, in
tolerable repair; one log stable, 15 feet by 12 feet, in
very bad repair; one barn and hay house, 40 feet by 24
feet, in good repair; one barn and hay house, 24 feet by 18
feet in bad repair; one Negro quarter, 24 feet by 18 feet,
in bad repair; and, an orchard with 180 thriving apple
trees; all valued at 40 pounds yearly. Signed by JOHN LEE
GIBSON and THOMAS GILES on January 20, 1798, and verified
by Justice JACOB FORWOOD on February 5, 1798.

The heirs of JAMES RIGBIE, deceased, verified that they had
received their dividends and settled the estate with
WILLIAM SMITH, executor or administrator of JAMES RIGBIE,
deceased, on April 6, 1798. Signed by JOSEPH BRINTON,
CASSANDRA CONSE (?), SAMUEL WALLIS, WILLIAM COALE and
AQUILA MASSEY, and witnessed by JOS. TURNER.

Court bound WILLIAM DOOLEY REASON, age 18 on March 31, 1797, to
MATTHEW SNOWDY until he is 21 to learn the carpenter and
joiner's trade. Said Reason shall obey his master, etc.,
and shall also receive three months' schooling and, in lieu
of clothing, he shall be paid $12 a year. Signed: JACOB
FORWOOD and WILLIAM SMITH, Aug. 9, 1797.

On March 19, 1794, CHARLES DEVINE had bound his son CHARLES
DEVINE to HENRY RUFF (tanner) who has since died. The
widow, HANNAH RUFF, by law has assigned her rights to said
Charles over to WILLIAM BULL (tanner) who will now fulfill
the remaining part of that agreement. Signed by HANNAH RUFF
and WILLIAM BULL on November 29, 1797, and witnessed by
HENRY WATTERS and GODFREY WATTERS.

On October 19, 1797 THOMAS BOOBY, father of ELIZABETH BOOBY,
came into Court and bound his daughter to HERMON STUMP.
Said ELIZABETH BOOBY was 10 years old on August 12th, and
she was bound until age 16 to learn to read, and to receive
necessary clothing and diet during that term. Signed by
JOHN ARCHER and WILLIAM SMITH, Justices.

On June 3, 1787 (1797?) JOHN GREEN, administrator of JOHN GREEN,
deceased, distributed goods and chattels from John's estate
to JOSHUA GREEN (who received, in part, negroes James and
Tom, a Bible, and farm equipment) and to ANN GREEN (who

received, in part, negro Charlotte, livestock, and kitchen items) valued at around 98 lbs.

Indenture, dated January 7, 1797, involving ALEXANDER CATHERWOOD, son of JOHN CATHERWOOD, who bound himself by his own free will and with his father's consent, to be an apprentice to ROGERS STREET to be a blacksmith for a term of 3 years and 2 months. Said Catherwood shall obey his master, shall not play in taverns, shall not commit matrimony, etc., and in return shall receive said training, six month's schooling, and one good suit of clothes at the end of said term. Signed by ALEXANDER CATHERWOOD, JOHN CATHERWOOD, and ROGERS STREET, and witnessed by THOMAS STETONE (STELONE?), JOHN CREIGHTON, and Court Justices NICHOLAS DAY McCOMAS and N. SMITH.

On May 16, 1788, MARY EAGON acknowledged receipt of 13 lbs., 8 shillings and 3 pence from WILLIAM HITCHCOCK as part of her father's estate. Witnessed by JAMES BARTON.

On March 15, 1788, THOMAS JAMES acknowledged receipt of 14 pounds, 6 shillings and 5 pence from WILLIAM HITCHCOCK in full for SOLOMON EAGON's part of his father's estate. Witnessed by JOHN HUGHES, JR.

On December 9, 1789, CLEMENTINE EAGON acknowledged receipt of 14 pounds, 3 shillings and 3 pence from WILLIAM HITCHCOCK as her full part of her father's estate. Her mark was witnessed by AQUILA PARKER and JOHN RENSHAW.

Indenture, dated November 17, 1796, involving SARAH SMITH, daughter of CATHARINE SMITH of Deer Creek Hundred, who bound herself with the consent of her mother to THOMAS SCARBOROUGH to be his servant until age 16, said Sarah now being 7 years old as of August 12, 1796. Said Sarah shall obey her master and cause him no harm, etc., and in return shall be taught to read, write, knit, sew and spin. Signed by SARAH SMITH (her mark) and CATHARINE SMITH (her mark), in the presence of JOHN BARCLAY and JOSEPH SCARBOROUGH, and verified by ROBERT MORGAN.

HENRY RICHARDSON and SOLOMON PERKINS had been appointed by the Court to audit and settle all matters in dispute between the representatives of ALICE SIMS and SARAH COOK, administratrix of ROBERT COOK (and GEORGE ANDERSON). They examined vouchers for two sales made of the estate of ALICE SIMS, to wit: one returned by the administrators to the commissary dated May 18, 1780 and another produced by SAMUEL McKISSON dated November 18th (he being clerk and having given his deposition), both amounting to 26 pounds, 4 pence half-penny. All legal amounts adjusted and attested by the above. Signed by HENRY RICHARDSON and SOLOMON PERKINS on July 29, 1797.

Justice JACOB FORWOOD appointed JOHN COOLEY and ABRAHAM REES on September 23, 1796, to enter upon the plantation of JOSEPH GORREL, deceased. MARTIN TAYLOR GILBERT was now guardian of LAWSON GORREL, orphan son of JOSEPH GORREL, and the land and tenements were now in the possession of JOSEPH EWING, to wit: 40 acre farm, 18 acres being cleared and the rest under timber; log dwelling house, 18 feet by 24 feet, with two poplar floors, one stone chimney with two fireplaces, covered with shingles and nearly gone to decay, which the guardian must cover in about 3 years at the expense of the estate; one small meat house about 8 feet square, covered with clapboards and built about 4 years ago; cleared land consists of two fields separated by woodland and under tolerable fence. Value estimated at 18 pounds, 10 shillings per year. Signed by JOHN COOLEY and ABRAHAM REES (his mark) on October 8, 1796, and verified by JACOB FORWOOD on October 15, 1796. Court acknowledged receipt of 15 sh. from MARTIN TAYLOR GILBERT, guardian of LAWSON GORREL, orphan of JOSEPH GORREL, for paying for the valuation.

On August 22, 1796, SUSANNA HUGHES acknowledged receipt of 44 pounds, 4 shillings and 3 pence from THOMAS HAYSE (HAYES), executor of CHARLES HUGHES, as part of her father's estate. Signed by SUSANNAH HUGHES (her mark) and witnessed by SAMUEL HUGHES and CHARLES ROCKHOLD.

On November 3, 1790, SAMSON EAGON acknowledged receipt of his full share of his father's estate from WILLIAM HITCHCOCK (amount not stated; year is clearly 1790).

On September 4, 1797, ELIZABETH MATHEWS acknowledged receipt from her uncle and guardian, JOHN DAY, the full amount of the inventory due her. Witness: NICHOLAS GASSAWAY.

On January 31, 1791 (date partially smudged - might be 1798 instead of 1791) ANN MATHEWS acknowledged receipt from CAPT. BENNETT MATHEWS of all articles inventoried except one ox main and one pair of steely yards.

Indenture, dated October 22, 1796 involving ELEANOR BURKINS who bound her son CHARLES BURKINS (with his consent) to JOHN FORWOOD until he arrives at age 21 (which will be on April 19, 1804) to be an apprentice in the farming business. Said Burkins shall obey his master, etc., and in return shall receive training and to learn to read, write and cipher as far as the rule of three, and at term's end, he shall receive a new suit of apparel. Signed by CHARLES BURKINS (his mark), ELEANOR BURKINS (her mark) and JOHN FORWOOD, in the presence of EDWARD PRALL and JOHN BARCLAY. (BURKINS also spelled BURKIN)

On March 17, 1797, WILLIAM ANDERSON, guardian of ARCHIBALD COOPER, consented to said Archibald serving his uncle, JAMES COOPER, for a term of 5 years as an apprentice to learn the blacksmith's trade, and to receive 10 months' schooling during the first year and 6 weeks' schooling each year afterwards, and to receive 2 suits of apparel at term's end, one of which suits must be new.

Indenture, dated June 20, 1794, involving JOHN WILSON (alias WELCH) who bound himself with the consent of his father to THOMAS STEPHENSON (STEVENSON) for a term of 8 years and 3 months to learn the cooper's trade. Said Wilson shall obey his master, not commit fornication, not get married, not haunt taverns, etc. and in return he shall receive training as a cooper and one year's schooling, and at the term's end

a good suit of apparel entirely new. Signed by JOHN
WILSON, JAMES WILSON, and THOMAS STEPHENSON. Witness: JOHN
BARCLAY and SAMUEL McKISSON.

On January 16, 1786, PATRICK CRETIN acknowledged that he had
received negro men named Jim (aged 39 years) and Natt, and,
on August 20, 1784, two cows and a filly. Total value: 137
lbs. All from the estate of JOHN CRETIN.

Indenture, dated March 19, 1794, involving CHARLES DEVINE who
bound his son CHARLES DEVINE as an apprentice to HENRY RUFF
to learn the tanning and currying trade until he arrives at
age 21, said Charles now being 13 years old as of February
20, 1794. Said Charles shall obey his master, not absent
himself without permission, not haunt taverns or
playhouses, etc., and in return he shall receive training
and 15 months' schooling, with customary freedom due when
he arrives at the age of 21. Signed by CHARLES DEVINE (his
mark) and HENRY RUFF, in the presence of LEVEN MATHEWS and
ANN MATHEWS.

On August 5, 1795, WILLIAM B. GOULD acknowledged receipt of 3
pounds and 8 pence from BENJAMIN EVEREST, it being a full
amount due to him from his father's (?) estate.

On May 4, 1792, AQUILA MITCHELL acknowledged receipt of 40
pounds from BENJAMIN EVEREST, it being an amount due to him
for his part of his father's personal property.

On January 26, 1796, ISAAC WEBSTER acknowledged receipt of 30
pounds and 7 pence from BENJAMIN EVEREST, it being an
amount due to his wife, ANN WHITAKER, as a legacy of EDWARD
MITCHELL's estate and received for that purpose.

On February 1, 1793, SARAH EAGAN made her mark on a note to
WILLIAM HITCHCOCK in which she asked him to let THOMAS
JAMES have her part of her father's estate "and in so doing
you will oblidge your friend." Wit: SAMSON EAGAN.

(ED. NOTE: Harford County, MD was not formed from Baltimore
County until 1773 and the government was not in place until
March, 1774. It is curious to see the following six entries
dated prior to that time and entered into the Orphans Court
Proceedings of Harford County. There were no reasons given
for these early entries. They do contain some very
important genealogical information that very possibly might
not be found anywhere else.)

On May 22, 1769, DANIEL HOWEL acknowledged receipt of one
shilling from WILLIAM VERCHWORTH, it being an amount "my
father thought proper to leave me by his will."

On August 20, 1769, FRANCIS BILLINGSLEY acknowledged (by his
mark) that he received one cow and calf, one horse, and one
negro boy from the estate of SAMUEL HOWEL, dec'd.

On November 10, 1770, WILLIAM GRAFTON, ROBERT JEWEL and SAMUEL
GRAFTON acknowledged receipt of one cow and calf from
WILLIAM VERCHWORTH "which their grandfather SAMUEL HOWEL

pleased to leave in his last will and testament."
Witnesses: JOHN SUDUK, SAMUEL HOWEL, ABERILLER HOWEL.

On January 11, 1773, ABERILLER HOWEL acknowledged receipt of two
negro boys named TONEY and JACOB, "being legacies left by
her father, SAMUEL HOWEL, as appeared by his last will and
testament, and appears by inventory of said estate to have
been appraised as viz., negro TONEY at 30 pounds, and negro
JACOB at 20 pounds. Signed by ABERILLER HOWEL. (No
witnesses to her signature)

On March 10, 1773, ABERILLER HOWEL acknowledged receipt from
WILLIAM VERCHWORTH of three bonds from THOMAS BOYLE "to her
late father, SAMUEL HOWEL, dated 11 & 12, 1764 for 59
pounds each, No. 1, 2 & 3, which were legacies left by her
father." Signed by ABERILLER HOWEL (No witness).

On March 1, 1773, ABERILLER HOWEL acknowledged receipt from
WILLIAM VERCHWORTH "all the lands left her as a legacy by
the will of her late father, SAMUEL HOWEL." Signed by
ABERILLER HOWEL. (No witnesses her to signature).

On February 16, 1789 MICAJAH MITCHELL and ABERILLER MITCHELL
reported in court: "Be it known to all it may concern that
I intermarried with a certain ABERILIA HOWEL, daughter of
SAMUEL HOWEL, deceased, and that I received some years back
from this date (from) Mr. WILLIAM VETCHWORTH, who
intermarried with the widow of said SAMUEL HOWEL, full
satisfaction for the said Aberila's fortune left her by her
said father." Signed by said MICAJAH MITCHELL and ABERILLER
MITCHELL in the presence of DAVID CLARK and JAMES BELL on
February 16, 1789.

On August 16, 1792, SAMUEL HOWEL acknowledged receipt from
"WILLIAM VERCHWORTH, who intermarried with my mother,
full satisfaction for my part of the estate left by my
father, SAMUEL HOWEL, deceased. Signed by SAMUEL HOWEL and
witnessed by ISAAC DAWS on August 16, 1792.

A Distribution of Negroes belonging to JOHN CRETIN, dec'd.,
between the widow ELIZABETH CRETIN and the children of the
deceased agreeable to his will, done on January 16, 1786 by
JOSEPH BROWNLEY and JOHN ARCHER. To ELIZABETH CRETIN,
negroes RACHEL, JIM, JO, RACHEL and MARY (value of 200
lbs.); to PATRICK CRETIN, negroes NAT and JIM (value of 115
lbs.); to JAMES CRETIN, negroes GEORGE and BETT (value of
100 lbs.); to JOHN CRETIN, negroes TOM and JUDE (valued of
140 lbs.); and, to ELIZABETH McCHERRY, negro Harry (value
of 27 lbs.) The difference in the dividend of negroes was
mutually paid out to all parties (adding up to a total
distribution of 582 lbs.) Receipt acknowledged by the widow
ELIZABETH CRETIN and the children: PATRICK CRETIN, JAMES
CRETIN, JOHN CRETIN and ELIZABETH McCHERRY (McSHERRY) on
August 20, 1792.

On October 21, 1790, JESSE BUSSEY acknowledged receipt from
WILLIAM HOLLIS, administrator of WILLIAM HOLLIS, "the sum
of 47 pounds specie in part of a balance of the estate due
to JESSE BUSSEY on account of his wife's third's part of
the estate." Witness: JACOB FORWOOD.

On March 10, 1797, SALLY COOPER acknowledged receipt from HENRY
    GREEN, guardian, the sum of 15 pounds due to her from her
    father LEONARD GREEN's estate.   Signed by SALLY COOPER and
    witnessed by BENNETT BUSSEY.

On December 8, 17--(year smudged and not legible), SOLOMON EAGON
    acknowledged receipt from ABRAHAM REESE, his guardian, the
    full share of his father SAMSON EAGON's estate, and having
    arrived at full age, said Reese is discharged from his
    guardianship. Signed by SOLOMON EAGON and witnessed by
    DANIEL KENLY and WILLIAM CREAL.

INDEX

92

Other books by the author:

Marylanders to Kentucky, 1775-1825

Methodist Records of Baltimore City, Maryland: Volume 1, 1799-1829

Methodist Records of Baltimore City, Maryland: Volume 2, 1830-1839

*Methodist Records of Baltimore City, Maryland: Volume 3, 1840-1850
(East City Station)*

More Maryland Deponents, 1716-1799

*More Marylanders to Carolina: Migration of Marylanders to
North Carolina and South Carolina prior to 1800*

More Marylanders to Kentucky, 1778-1828

Outpensioners of Harford County, Maryland, 1856-1896

Presbyterian Records of Baltimore City, Maryland, 1765-1840

Quaker Records of Baltimore and Harford Counties, Maryland, 1801-1825

Quaker Records of Northern Maryland, 1716-1800

Quaker Records of Southern Maryland, 1658-1800

Revolutionary Patriots of Anne Arundel County, Maryland

Revolutionary Patriots of Baltimore Town and Baltimore County, 1775-1783

Revolutionary Patriots of Calvert and St. Mary's Counties, Maryland, 1775-1783

Revolutionary Patriots of Caroline County, Maryland, 1775-1783

Revolutionary Patriots of Cecil County, Maryland

Revolutionary Patriots of Charles County, Maryland, 1775-1783

Revolutionary Patriots of Delaware, 1775-1783

Revolutionary Patriots of Dorchester County, Maryland, 1775-1783

Revolutionary Patriots of Frederick County, Maryland, 1775-1783

Revolutionary Patriots of Harford County, Maryland, 1775-1783

Revolutionary Patriots of Kent and Queen Anne's Counties

Revolutionary Patriots of Lancaster County, Pennsylvania

Revolutionary Patriots of Maryland, 1775-1783: A Supplement

Revolutionary Patriots of Maryland, 1775-1783: Second Supplement

Revolutionary Patriots of Montgomery County, Maryland, 1776-1783

Revolutionary Patriots of Prince George's County, Maryland, 1775-1783

Revolutionary Patriots of Talbot County, Maryland, 1775-1783

Revolutionary Patriots of Worcester and Somerset Counties, Maryland, 1775-1783

Revolutionary Patriots of Washington County, Maryland, 1776-1783

*St. George's (Old Spesutia) Parish, Harford County, Maryland:
Church and Cemetery Records, 1820-1920*

St. John's and St. George's Parish Registers, 1696-1851

Survey Field Book of David and William Clark in Harford County, Maryland, 1770-1812

The Crenshaws of Kentucky, 1800-1995

The Delaware Militia in the War of 1812

*Union Chapel United Methodist Church Cemetery Tombstone Inscriptions,
Wilna, Harford County, Maryland*

www.ingramcontent.com/pod-product-compliance
Lightning Source LLC
LaVergne TN
LVHW021610080426
835510LV00019B/2509